THE
ULTIMATE GUIDE
TO BEING A

SUPERHERO

WARNING: KEEP THIS BOOK SAFE FROM VILLAINS

Owing to the important and secret nature of this volume, do not—repeat: DO NOT—let this book fall into the hands of villains. We recommend the following precautions be taken during your possession:

DISGUISE YOUR BOOK WITH A FAKE BOOK COVER (PREFERABLY SOMETHING BORING, LIKE 17TH-CENTURY FRENCH POETRY).

KEEP IT HIDDEN IN A SAFE PLACE, LIKE IN YOUR UNDERWEAR DRAWER. (NO VILLAIN WILL EVER LOOK THERE.)

CHOOSE A TOP SECRET LOCATION TO STUDY THE MANUAL, AND KEEP AN EYE OUT FOR SPYING VILLAINS.

CHANGE HIDING PLACES OFTEN SO IT'S HARDER FOR A VILLAIN TO TRACK THE BOOK DOWN AND STEAL IT.

This book is for SUPERS ONLY! Villains, henchmen, henchwomen, hench-pets, robots, and aliens of all kinds found possessing this book will be PROSECUTED. (At least, we'll be very, very angry and won't feature you in the next edition.)

Copyright © 2016 by Barbara Beery, Brooke Jorden, and David Miles
Illustrations copyright © 2016 by Jeff Harvey
All rights reserved.

Published by Familius LLC, www.familius.com

Familius books are available at special discounts for bulk purchases, whether for sales promotions or for family or corporate use. For more information, contact Familius Sales at 559-876-2170 or email orders@familius.com.

Library of Congress Cataloging-in-Publication Data   2015955943   ISBN 9781942934455

Edited by Adam McClain and Sarah Echard
Recipe photography by Victoria Leonardo and Lisette Donado
Craft photography by David Miles and Stephanie Cleveland
Cartoon illustrations on pages 12, 21, 40-51, 60, 65, 83, 90, 100, 128, 136, 142-143, 150 by Jeff Harvey
All other photography and graphic elements used or adapted from Shutterstock.com
Cover and book design by David Miles

10 9 8 7 6 5 4 3 2 1

First Edition   Printed in China

THE
ULTIMATE GUIDE

TO BEING A

101
SUPERHERO

RECIPES,
MANEUVERS,
GADGETS
& TIPS

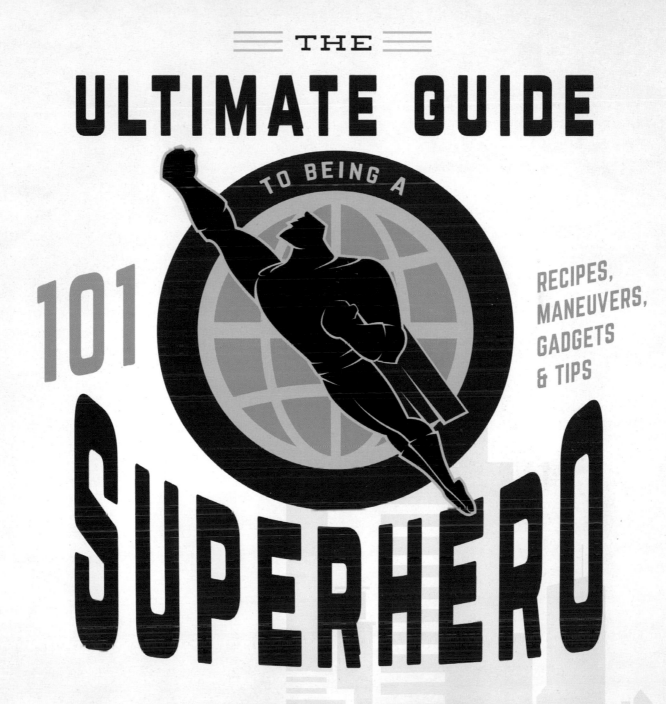

**A KID'S MANUAL FOR SAVING THE WORLD,
LOOKING GOOD IN SPANDEX, AND
GETTING HOME IN TIME FOR DINNER**

BARBARA BEERY

WITH **BROOKE JORDEN** AND **DAVID MILES**

Dear Superhero,

Welcome to *The Ultimate Guide to Being a Superhero*! Within these pages, you'll find all the tips, gadgets, recipes, and maneuvers you need to know to become a top-notch superhero and save the world.

Before you begin your journey to superherodom, there are a few items we should mention:

Don't Try This at Home

Some of the maneuvers in the book are merely theoretical. Please do not attempt to leap from tall buildings, smash through brick walls, confront gamma radiation without protective eyewear, etc. This guide is for educational and informational purposes only and should not take the place of training by a licensed supermentor or plain old common sense.

Keep Your Fists of Fury in Check

While your little brother may deserve a clobbering, he probably isn't the most suitable punching bag. Save your karate chops and punches for the supervillains—or better yet, practice with an actual punching bag (see page 115 to make your own).

Parental Guidance Suggested

Superheroes are well acquainted with danger, but they should never be ashamed to ask for help. Some of the activities and stunts in this book may require the assistance of a parent or trusted adult, particularly those involving a hot stove, a hot glue gun, or cutting utensils. Let Mom or Dad come to the rescue and help you out with these not-so-safe tools.

With these considerations in mind, you are ready to become a full-fledged, crime-fighting, spandex-wearing superhero. Now get out there and save some lives!

Good luck!

MANUAL CONTENTS

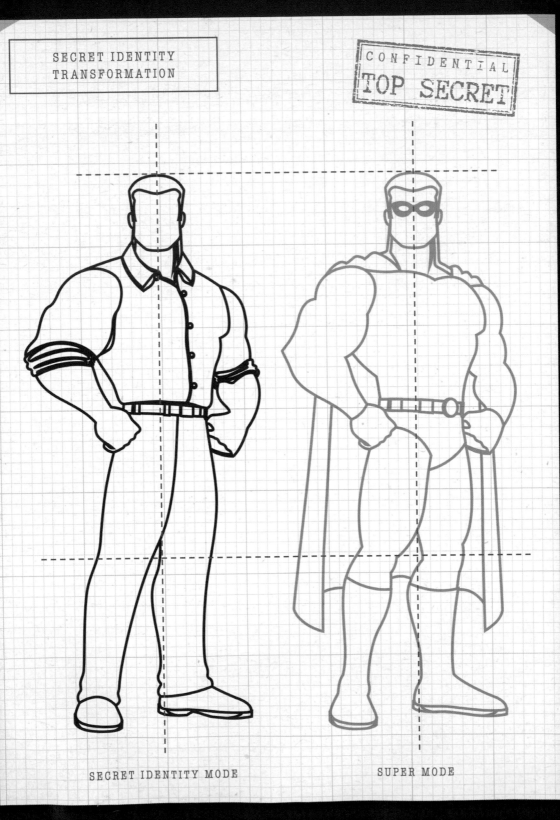

SECRET IDENTITY
TRANSFORMATION

CONFIDENTIAL
TOP SECRET

SECRET IDENTITY MODE

SUPER MODE

1

SECRET IDENTITY 101

SECRET IDENTITY

1A.1 PROTECTING YOUR MOST VALUABLE POSSESSION

As every superhero knows, your real identity is your most valuable possession. Not only does it protect you from harm, but it also protects your parents, family, friends, and favorite kindergarten teacher from being used as bait. Under no circumstances should you ever reveal your birth name, birthdate, social security number, or, for good measure, your childhood ice cream preferences.

CASE STUDY: TORNATOR

Tornator enjoyed 16 years as a celebrated crime-fighting hero. His career came to an abrupt end when he left his wallet at the local pizza parlor. Tornator—and the meat supreme pizza he was carrying—were never seen again. What a shame—it really was good pizza.

Villains pay good money to get their hands on a superhero's secret identity, but they aren't the only ones. Eager reporters and tabloid writers would do anything to unmask a famous hero. Needless to say, that would be disastrous to your career. Learn more about avoiding both reporters and photographers on page 20 and page 22.

EXCLUSIVE:

THE THUNDER IS UNMASKED

New York City—For years, Thunderwoman's trademark lighting has lit up the skyline of New York City as she went about her missions of mercy. Fans have heralded her good deeds, but from subways to coffee shops, one question has dominated the talk: Who is this mysterious do-gooder?

In this exclusive report, *The Chronicle* is pleased to report that Thunderwoman is none other than Angelina Roscow, the supermodel-turned-philanthropist wife of billionaire Tom Roscow. Roscow's

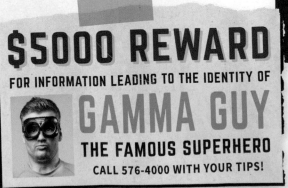

U.S. SUPER IDENTIFICATION STATUS UPDATE
LEVEL 1 SECURITY: NOT EVEN YOUR MOM CAN SEE THIS

The last year has brought a marked rise in the level of s... ...ed their
eff... ...deemed... ...e major
me... ...ntificat... ...udes 10
me... ...dle cla... ...lows.

the... ...the lev... ...creased
maj... ...'s as d... ...d in the
won... ...e iden... ...n and 5
...detail...

SUPER: QUANTUM

ALIAS: JIM MARCONE, BUSINESSMAN

Every government tries to keep tabs on those with superpowers. Though the feds are usually friendly partners, it's best to keep your identity a secret even from them . . . especially during election years.

SUPER: SHADOWGIRL

ALIAS: KIM JORDEN,
TELEMARKETER . . . IN TRAINING

1B THE MASK

1B.1 YOUR FIRST LINE OF DEFENSE

Masks are essential to protecting your identity, but they're also downright stylish. Let's face it: spandex tights can only look so great, so a well-designed mask is key to cutting a good figure out there.

OVERVIEW OF COMMON MASK STYLES

Mask fashion comes and goes, but most superheroes opt for one of several common styles.

CLASSIC

An oldie but a goodie. Flexible, durable, and breathes great during combat.

EAGLE EYES

A trendy take on the classic. Features sharper curves and angles. Best for dinner parties and formal occasions.

NINJA WRAP

As comfortable as the classic, but less likely to fall off during combat.

METAL MASK

Incredibly uncomfortable but extremely durable and flameproof.

VISOR VISION

Harder to breathe through but great at covering telltale moles and scars that might give your identity away.

THEATRIC

Highly impractical. Usually a dead giveaway that you're a either novice or slightly deranged, neither of which is good.

HOW TO MODIFY YOUR MASK FOR INCLEMENT CONDITIONS

RAIN

Adding a plastic covering over the eyeholes can be helpful, especially on long flights.

WIND

An extra-wide strap can help keep your mask in place. You might also want to tighten the band more than usual.

SNOW / ICE

Since most of your heat is lost through your head, adapting your usual mask into a ninja wrap might be a good cold-weather option.

TIME TRAVEL

If you're going back in time by more than 50 years, you'll want to pick a fabric that blends in with superheroes of that age. Silk is usually a safe bet for most eras before 1900.

FROM THE FILES OF
CHRISTOPHER CARDALL
FOUNDER, SUPERHERO DESIGNER FASHION

SUPERHERO MASK DESIGN 101

COVERAGE

Should cover at least 40% of super's face for minimum concealment of identity.

QUALITY MATERIAL

Material should be flame retardant, flexible, and breathable to prevent chafing. Wrinkle-free and stain resistant is also ideal.

EYE OPENINGS

Make large enough to maximize visibility, but small enough to hide identity and protect eyes from sharp objects and bird droppings.

DURABLE BAND

Keep this strong and secure so the mask doesn't fly off when super is flying at Mach 5.

EXPOSED NOSE

Preferred for maximum respiration.

CC | TEXTILE COLORS

CC147 FLAME RED	CC136 ATLANTIS BLUE
CC146 NUCLEAR CORE	CC137 URANUS
CC145 GOLD	CC138 MICROBIAL
CC144 WEATHERED ARMOR	CC139 SWAMP MOSS

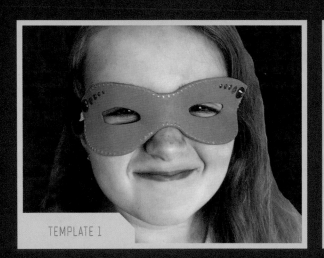

TEMPLATE 1

TEMPLATE 2

 ## 18.2 MAKE YOUR OWN SUPERHERO MASK

Protect your anonymity with a classic superhero mask. (On a side note, they are wonderfully comfortable.)

SUPPLIES:

Cardstock, cardboard, or craft foam

Scissors

Hole punch

Elastic string or elastic band

Crayons or markers

Glue

Glitter, sequins, foam stickers, felt; any and all superhero "bling"

MISSION:

Draw a mask shape on a piece of card stock, cardboard, or craft foam. (If you need help getting the right shape, you can photocopy or trace one of the templates to the right.) Cut out the mask, then ask an adult to help cut out the eyeholes for you.

Using a hold punch, cut a pair of holes, one of each side of the mask. Cut a length of elastic string (about 12 inches long) and tie one end through each hole.

Color your mask. Decorate with glitter, sequins, foam stickers, etc. Allow to dry completely before trying on.

Slip on your superhero mask. (It should fit snugly but not too tight.) Adjust the length of the elastic if necessary so you are comfortable and well disguised.

Save the world!

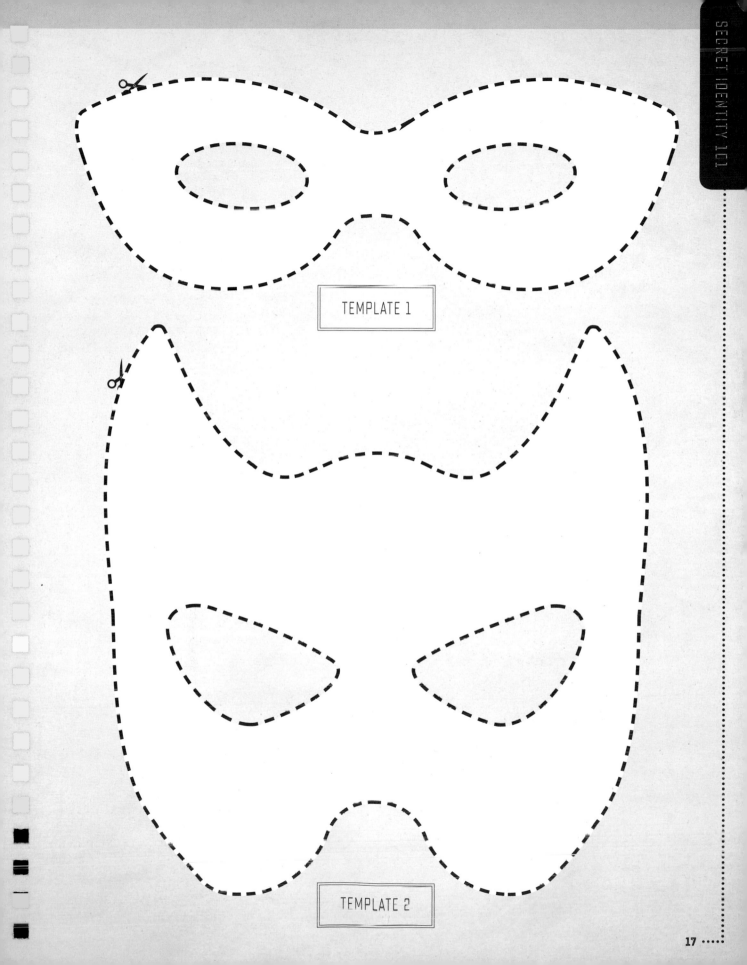

TEMPLATE 1

TEMPLATE 2

Aldente (alias: Chef Giuseppi) safeguarded the cities of Naples and Rome for over a decade. Though known among villains for his odd martial arts style (affectionately called "the meat grinder"), he is best known among superheroes for his delicious contributions to superhero cuisine, including Power-Boosting Smoothies (page 126), Bam! Burrito Bowls (page 109), and the Secret Identity Sandwiches, featured here. If you ever take him to lunch, you'd better order the pasta.

18.3 SECRET IDENTITY SANDWICHES

Delicious and particularly popular at superhero potlucks, the Secret Identity Sandwich packs powerful nutrients from hummus, carrots, and spinach.

SUPPLIES:

1 sun-dried tomato wrap

2 spinach wraps

1/2 cup hummus

1/8 cup baby spinach

1/8 cup shredded carrot

1/8 cup shredded cheese

Salt and pepper, to taste

1 hard boiled egg, sliced

1 cherry tomato, sliced

1 black olive, halved

Spinach is packed with vitamins A and K and tons of other nutrients. It's a favorite among superheroes—and luckily, villains NEVER eat their veggies.

MISSION:

1 Cut each sun-dried tomato and spinach wrap into an oval shape of equal size.

2 Carefully cut away the lower third of the sun-dried tomato wrap in a wavy pattern that resembles the bottom of a mask. Discard. Then, using a 3- to 4-inch mask-shaped cookie cutter (or plain circles, if you prefer), cut out eyeholes in the sun-dried tomato wrap. Set aside until ready to use.

3 Spread the first spinach wrap with about half of the hummus. Sprinkle spinach, carrots, and cheese on top of the hummus and season with salt and pepper.

4 Place the second spinach wrap on top of the filling and press to hold together.

5 Spread the remaining hummus on the sun-dried tomato "mask," then place the mask hummus-side down on top of the spinach wrap. Press to hold everything togther.

6 Set 1 egg slice into each eye opening of the mask cutout. Top each egg slice with a slice of cherry tomato and 1/2 black olive.

7 Decorate with leftover wrap cutouts, cheese cutouts, and other veggies.

MAKES 1

1C AVOIDING DETECTION

1C.1 HOW TO HANDLE A REPORTER

You've stopped the hurricane, disarmed the nuclear missile, and negotiated a peace treaty with the invading alien species. But don't let your guard down, because your biggest challenge is headed your way: the hoard of reporters. Reporters are snoops of the worst degree, and nothing drives one mad like not knowing the real identity of a national hero. Remember that what begins as a friendly interview for the 5 o'clock news can quickly turn into an identity crisis of mammoth proportions. Our advice? Save your tales of glory for the annual superhero Christmas party and avoid all contact with reporters like they're a Kryptonite Cupcake (see page 62).

If opting for #4, you might want to keep a fan club badge on hand at all times.

IF YOU DO FIND YOURSELF ENTANGLED IN A REPORTER CRISIS, HERE ARE FOUR SURE-FIRE WAYS TO MAKE A QUICK GETAWAY.

1 Yell, "Watch out! Invading pink bunnies from outer space!" and dash off while everyone is looking up.

2 Ask the interviewer, "I'm sorry, but is that a wig you're wearing?" on national television. Not only will this thoroughly derail the interview, but it will ensure other reporters steer clear of you for weeks.

3 Discreetly melt the camera lens while no one is looking. If you aren't equipped with laser vision, a well-placed whiplash sneeze right into the lens will do the trick. You won't get many points for style, but it does get the job done (and you might just slime the reporter to boot. Sorry, not sorry?).

4 Pretend you're just a member of the fan club in costume who got mistaken for the real thing. Shouting "Trick or treat!" might help, but if you look like a mountain of muscle, we recommend options 1–3 instead.

1C.2 DEALING WITH FRIENDS AND FAMILY

Your family means well, but it's best not to let them in on your secret superhero service. The more they know, the more danger you and they will both be in. Besides, even the most understanding mom is going to make you make your bed before you leave the house, evil world domination plot notwithstanding.

HANDY EXCUSES:

Whether it is an explosion or an alien invasion, when disaster strikes, the world will need you. But if you always run off during dangerous situations, your friends and family members might start to get a little suspicious. Keep a notebook of convenient excuses that you can turn to when you need to get off the hook.

I FORGOT MY GLASSES.

I THOUGHT I LEFT THE OVEN ON.

I HAD TO TAKE A PHONE CALL.

I WAS REALLY CRAVING A CHEESEBURGER.

I THOUGHT I SAW [INSERT YOUR FAVORITE CELEBRITY].

I HAD JURY DUTY.

I REALLY HAD TO USE THE BATHROOM.

I'M ALLERGIC TO ALIENS.

You might want some extra excuses on hand for your toughest customers:

NO. 37

SUBSTITUTE TEACHER

SAY: "I think I'm going to throw up."

NO. 4

OLDER SISTER

SAY: "Let me go, or I'll tell Mom about the time you _____."

NO. 29

GROUCHY NEIGHBOR

SAY: "Look, someone's dog is peeing in your yard!" (then run off)

1C.3 HOW TO EVADE A PHOTOGRAPHER

Photographers won't ask you pesky questions, but they can be more dangerous than the average reporter. To keep one from snapping a mugshot of your secret identity, be sure you change in and out of your supersuit in secure, secret locations (see page 24).

IF AN UNUSUALLY DETERMINED PHOTOGRAPHER IS ON YOUR TRAIL, HERE ARE FOUR WAYS TO THROW HIM OR HER OFF:

1 Zig zag. Doubling back through a sewage treatment plant or military parade can be especially effective.

2 Shout, "Look! A rare Sumatran Rhinoceros!" and run. The one thing photographers want more than a picture of you is a chance to be on the cover of *National Geographic*.

3 Casually mention that you used to eat photographers for breakfast. You're now a vegan, but . . .

4 Sing a campfire song from Camp Super (see page 128). Even the worst photographer won't be able to stand that for long.

SPOT THE PHOTOGRAPHER

Your flat might seem secure, but it's vital to check the grounds for photographers. The pests can hide more places than you realize.

1 Clinging to the top of the tree

2 Peeking in at the window blinds

3 Waiting to sneak through the gate behind your car

4 Crouching on the top of the roof

5 Hiding behind the stone wall

6 Peering around the corner

SAFE HOUSE #CA67-8

WEASEL

OCTOBER 23, 1959 | VOL. 66

15¢

Mighty Girl spotted at local gym
pg. 15

EXPOSED!

ACTIVIST JOHN STEEL CAUGHT BECOMING

GAMMA GUY! pg. 46

IS BILLIONAIRE MCCOY WALTON REALLY THE HAMMER?
pg. 32

Watch out! Tabloids will pay photographers big bucks for your mug. Save your photo for a Wheaties box.

10 CHANGING INTO YOUR SUPERSUIT

10.1 THERE'S A TIME TO CHANGE . . . AND A TIME NOT TO CHANGE

The most uncomfortable part of a superhero's life—apart from the spandex itself—is finding suitable places to change into your supersuit. Superheroes have used the following staples for years:

TELEPHONE BOOTHS

The obvious choice.

LARGE SHRUBS

But avoid rosebushes.

TAXI CABS

Not as much privacy, but ideal if you're on the go.

GRANDMA'S HOUSE

Free cookies included!

ELEVATORS

If you're slow at changing, you might want to start it at the top floor first.

DUMPSTERS

Plentiful in large cities, but definitely your last resort.

✂ 10.2 MAKE YOUR OWN PHONE BOOTH

BOX 2, GLUED AND TRIMMED TO 4" TALL

SUPPLIES:

2 large cardboard boxes, both the same size (we recommend using wardrobe boxes for a small booth or refrigerator boxes for a large one)

Packaging tape

Hot glue gun and glue sticks

Ruler

Craft knife

1 pint red latex interior paint

Large paint brush

Glue stick

Paper, light blue and yellow

Stapler

Black craft foam

Painter's or electrical tape for decoration

BOX 1, FLAPS OPENED AND TAPED

MISSION:

1. Open the top and bottom flaps of one cardboard box. Use packaging tape to secure the flaps in an open position, creating a tall column that is open at either end.

    🏃 **TIP: If possible, use packaging tape that has a matte finish instead of glossy. The paint will stick better later on.**

2. Use the second cardboard box as a cap to stabilize the structure. To do this, carefully hot glue the flaps closed on one end of the second box. Cut the box down to about 4 inches tall and fit the cap onto the phone booth.

3. Plan where to put the door, preferably at least 4 inches from the top and sides of the box. Cut the top and one side of the door into the box. On the inside of the box, use a craft knife to score the remaining edge of the door. This will help the door open and close easier.

4. Paint the phone booth and let it dry.

    🏃 **TIP: Cardboard absorbs paint, so you might need several coats to get a solid finish.**

5. Use a glue stick to attach squares of blue paper in a grid pattern to resemble windows.

6. Print or write the word "Telephone" on a strip of yellow paper and glue it to the top.

7. Use painter's or electrical tape to embellish your phone booth and give the windows depth.

8. Staple a strip of black craft foam to the open side of the door to serve as a handle.

CC

SHIRT #FK8-2

CAPE #KJ9-1

VISOR #KD-13

CHRISTOPHER CARDALL

FOUNDER
SUPERHERO DESIGNER FASHION
202.555.0187

10.3 PRESTO-CHANGE-O COOKIES

Superheroes' outfits define who they are to the world. Red and blue mean powerful and loyal. Black and yellow mean mysterious and shadowed. What will your cookies say about you? Think it through before taking them to the next Superhero Charity Bake Sale.

SUPPLIES:

1/2 cup (1 stick) butter, room temperature

3/4 cup sugar

1 egg

1 teaspoon vanilla

2 cups flour

1/2 teaspoon baking soda

1/4 teaspoon salt

Purchased icing

Assorted food colorings and candy decorations

MISSION:

1 Preheat oven to 375 degrees. Line two cookie sheets with foil or parchment paper. Place decorations in a small bowl. Set aside until ready to use.

2 Cream butter in a large mixing bowl with a mixer. Slowly add sugar, beating until light and fluffy. Add egg and vanilla, mixing well.

3 Combine flour, soda, and salt in a separate bowl. Add to creamed mixture, blending well. Dough will be very stiff.

4 Roll out dough on lightly floured surface and out into shapes. Bake for 8 to 10 minutes or until lightly browned. Remove from oven and cool on wire racks 5 minutes before removing to cool completely. Frost and decorate.

MAKES ABOUT 12 3-INCH COOKIES

CIVILIAN PROFILE: CHRISTOPHER CARDALL

Though not a super, the boy genius Christopher Cardall is invaluable to the superhero community. With the mind of an Edison and the eye of a Michelangelo, Cardall has created a signature line of superhero outfits and gear that leave villains mute with envy. He is best known for his functional Wrist Cuffs (see page 77), his Super Speed Grip Socks (see page 88), and his widespread theories on supersuit design (see page 72).

1E CHOOSING YOUR SECRET IDENTITY

1E.1 CLASSIC ALIAS CHOICES

To protect the people you care about, it is vital that you maintain a secret identity. And besides, you can't walk around in tights all day every day. Here are a few popular choices:

PASSPORT

Superheroes Anonymous

PHOTOGRAPHER

PROS:	Opportunity to snap a selfie of your heroic deeds; friends think you're "artistic"; secret hideout can double as darkroom
CONS:	Small salary (like, really small); questionable job security; Mom will always ask you to document family reunions
SUPERHEROES CURRENTLY USING:	Aperture, Focus, Shutter Speed

MILD-MANNERED JOURNALIST

PROS:	Press pass for any emergency; inside scoop on what the media really knows about you; opportunities to meet and interview interesting people
CONS:	Demanding hours; picky editors; cutthroat, er, competitive work environment
SUPERHEROES CURRENTLY USING:	The Scrivener, Captain Caption, Masthead

SECURE ALIAS SELECTION
PREPARED BY G. S. JOHNSON, COUNSEL

WEALTHY BUSINESS TYCOON

PROS: Inexhaustible wealth; private jet; spacious mansion

CONS: Must keep up public appearances; exhausting parties; bored, er, board meetings

SUPERHEROES CURRENTLY USING: Nimbus, Dr. Dividend, Blue Chip

PROS: Potential to inspire young minds; full access to laboratory equipment and chemicals; summer vacation

CONS: Risk of exposure to radioactive chemicals; grading (and actually reading) student papers; "nerd" status

SUPERHEROES Gallium Girl, Antimony, Thorium

CHEMISTRY PROFESSOR

PIZZA DELIVERY SPECIALIST

PROS: Free food; access to transportation (bicycle, car, etc.)

CONS: Uniform that makes spandex look classy; angry customers; possible weight gain (1 lap around the city burns 3 slices of pizza)

SUPERHEROES CURRENTLY USING: Caputo Kid, Cornicione, Miss Margherita

SECRET IDENTITY APTITUDE TEST

Select one answer for each of the questions below. Circle the corresponding number of points for each answer. When you're finished, add up your total points in the last column. Compare your total points to the "Scoring" table and see what secret identity is best for you!

QUESTION	SELECT YOUR ANSWER	POINTS
1 If you had a free afternoon, what would you most want to do?	Play video games.	1
	Go to the library.	(2)
	Take a walk in the park.	3
	Visit the bank.	4
	Rent a movie.	5
2 What's your dream home?	An apartment, away from your parents.	1
	A brick house with a large study.	(2)
	A condo downtown in the city.	3
	A 200-year-old mansion.	4
	A glamorous yacht.	5
3 Preferred transportation?	A used car.	1
	A bicycle.	(2)
	The train or subway.	3
	A touring car with chrome and leather.	4
	A sleek, black limo.	5
4 What's your favorite subject in school?	I skipped school.	1
	Chemistry.	2
	English.	(3)
	Economics.	4
	Drama.	5
5 If you could meet anyone, who would it be?	The Ninja Turtles.	1
	Albert Einstein.	(2)
	The President of the United States.	3
	Donald Trump.	4
	Mickey Mouse.	5

QUESTION	SELECT YOUR ANSWER	POINTS
6 What do you want most for Christmas?	A year's supply of pepperoni.	1
	An electron microscope.	2
	The latest new camera.	3
	A statue of George Washington.	(4)
	Diamonds, of course.	5
7 Favorite type of TV show?	Cartoons.	(1)
	Nature shows.	2
	The news.	3
	Stock market reports.	4
	Soap operas.	5
8 Place you most want to visit?	Italy.	1
	Germany.	2
	London.	3
	New York City.	(4)
	Los Angeles.	5

YOUR TOTAL POINTS (20)

SCORING

0-8	9-16	17-24	25-32	33-40
Pizza Delivery Specialist	Chemistry Professor	Journalist/ Photographer	Wealthy Business Tycoon	Hollywood Actor

1E.3 MAKE YOUR OWN IDENTITY CARDS

If someone questions your alias, it's always helpful to have an "official" ID badge you can flash their way. Show it just long enough to dispel any questions, then make a quick—but natural—getaway.

SUPPLIES:

Computer paper	A photo of you
Cardstock or thin cardboard	ID badge lanyard

MISSION:

1 Have your parents help you make photocopies of these pages. You won't want to ruin your manual!

2 Cut out the photocopied cards and glue them onto cardstock or cardboard. (Tip: A used cereal box works great, too.) Trim off the extra cardboard.

3 Have your parents help you make some photocopies or printouts of your photograph. Cut them into squares, and glue them onto the photo spots indicated on the cards. Attach your card to an official lanyard.

The **Enquirer**

OFFICAL PHOTOGRAPHER'S PASS

NAME

ID NO. 4982

GLUE PHOTO HERE

★ PREMIUM ★
PIZZA
1915

LICENSED DELIVERY SPECIALIST

NAME

DRIVER ID NUMBER: 39HJ1

PIZZA DELIVERY SPECIALIST

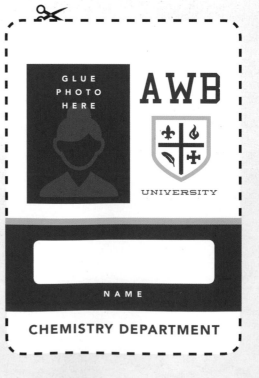

GLUE PHOTO HERE

AWB

UNIVERSITY

NAME

CHEMISTRY DEPARTMENT

CHEMISTRY PROFESSOR

GLUE PHOTO HERE

5 news

Channel 5 News

NAME

Field Reporter

MILD-MANNERED JOURNALIST

GLUE PHOTO HERE

The Enquirer

OFFICAL PHOTOGRAPHER'S PASS

NAME

ID NO. 4982

PHOTOGRAPHER

GLUE PHOTO HERE

ACME Industries

165 Business Ave.
Commerce, US 19821

NAME

LEVEL 1 CLEARANCE

WEALTHY BUSINESS TYCOON

GLUE PHOTO HERE

GMG

BACKLOT ACCESS

NAME

MUST BE RENEWED IN 6 MONTHS

HOLLYWOOD ACTOR

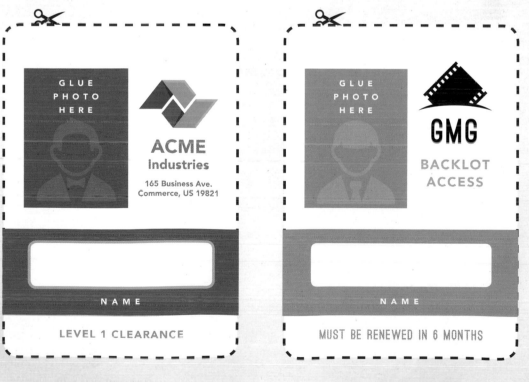

1E.4 DINNER IN DISGUISE

Disguise isn't always just for your identity. These tasty morsels have been delighting superheroes (and baffling villains) since their debut at the Super Expo in 1973.

SUPPLIES:

1 pound lean ground turkey

1/2 cup bread crumbs

1 cup grated Monterey jack cheese

1 tablespoon Worcestershire sauce

3 tablespoons ketchup

1 egg

3 cups mashed potatoes

Assorted paste food colorings (optional)

MISSION:

1 Preheat oven to 375 degrees. Line 12 muffin tin cups with foil baking cups.

2 In a large bowl, mix together all ingredients except the mashed potatoes and food coloring until well combined.

3 Divide the mixture evenly among the lined cups (about 3/4 full).

4 Bake for approximately 15 minutes or until cooked through. Remove from oven to cool slightly.

5 If you choose to color the frosting, divide the mashed potatoes among three small bowls and stir in a few drops of food coloring to each.

6 Frost each cupcake with different colors of mashed potato frosting and serve.

MAKES 12

Recommended condiments:

ketchup

Mustard

IDEA: CHERRY TOMATO

IDEA: BELL PEPPER SPRINKLES

MASHED POTATO FROSTING

MEAT LOAF CAKE

CONFIDENTIAL TOP SECRET

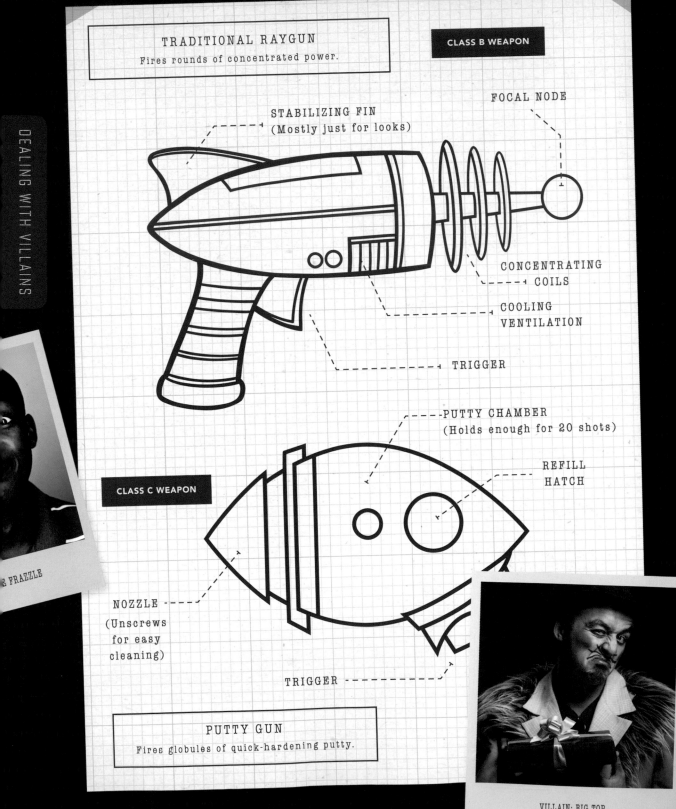

TRADITIONAL RAYGUN
Fires rounds of concentrated power.

CLASS B WEAPON

STABILIZING FIN
(Mostly just for looks)

FOCAL NODE

CONCENTRATING
COILS

COOLING
VENTILATION

TRIGGER

PUTTY CHAMBER
(Holds enough for 20 shots)

REFILL
HATCH

CLASS C WEAPON

NOZZLE
(Unscrews
for easy
cleaning)

TRIGGER

PUTTY GUN
Fires globules of quick-hardening putty.

E FRAZZLE

VILLAIN: BIG TOP

2

DEALING WITH VILLAINS

2A FIGHTING EVIL

2A.1 YOUR FIGHT

Superheroes represent all that is just and good, but their counterparts—super-villains—take a very different path. With supervillains loose in a city, you can be sure there is trouble brewing. Some villains are laughable, predictable, and even lovable (to a point); others are cunning, ruthless, and at times more than a hero can handle. So how can you prepare to face these villains? Knowledge. Learn what makes them tick. Learn how to spot their plots and disable their ray guns and avoid their traps. Know your enemy.

After all, what is a hero without a villain to defeat?

2A.2 HOW TO PICK YOUR NEMESIS

When choosing your super nemesis, it pays to be both patient and picky. Not every bad guy on the street will be a good match. Take some time to weigh the competition before declaring war on an enemy who may, ultimately, be less dangerous than a day-old tuna sandwich (and just as boring).

THE IDEAL NEMESIS SHOULD:

- ☐ Be completely, utterly, and thoroughly evil.
- ☐ Appreciate witty banter during face-offs.
- ☐ Wreak havoc on the city in which you live (i.e., short commute).
- ☐ Have the courtesy not to attack the city before 7 a.m.
- ☑ Be frighteningly powerful, yet fairly predictable.

And how do you let your nemesis know that he or she now has a nemesis?

OPTION 1: Foil your nemesis's sinister plots. (Probably the most obvious approach)

OPTION 2: Send your nemesis a strongly worded letter. (Your message will be clear *and* eloquent.)

OPTION 3: Intentionally mispronounce his or her name as many times as possible during a TV interview.

Remember, not every villain wears a mask and a carries a death ray. Some monsters are more difficult to spot because we see them every day. In fact, you might not think of these things as villains at all, but true heroes fight evil in all its forms. So what can you do to fight the everyday evil in life?

2A.3

FIGHTING EVERYDAY EVIL

FIGHT POLLUTION: Throw away trash you see on the ground.

FIGHT OVERGROWTH: Secretly pull your neighbor's weeds. (Weeds are the root of all evil!)

FIGHT INJUSTICE: Stand up to the bullies and defend the underdogs.

FIGHT MALNUTRITION: Eat your spinach. (Talk about superfood! See page 19.)

FIGHT MELANCHOLY: Smile at someone who's having a bad day.

FIGHT HALITOSIS: Floss. (Plaque is one enemy that doesn't stand a chance.)

FIGHT IGNORANCE: Learn something new every day. (Knowledge is power!)

Villains come from all walks of life but usually have one common objective: power (or at least giving you a really hard time).

VILLAIN PROFILE: THE TERMIGATOR

When an experiment in a genetics lab in the Florida wetlands went terribly wrong, mild-mannered research assistant Delmont Cotter was tragically transformed into the Termigator: half man, half gator, and all mean. He can hold his breath for up to twenty minutes, and his tough, scale-like armor, razor-sharp teeth, and beady little eyes have caused more than one superhero to need a change of spandex. His biggest pet peeve: being confused with Doc Croc.

VILLAIN PROFILE: THE PAJAMA MASTER

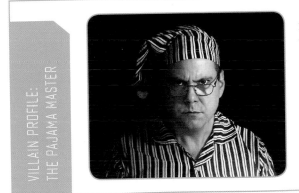

Forget Santa Claus—The Pajama Master sees you when you're sleeping and knows when you're awake. In his glory days, he raised an army of sleepwalkers to do his bidding by connecting their brains telepathically through sleep patterns. Somehow, he even managed to make footed one-piece pajamas and a nightcap look stylish! But after failing to build an army in Seattle (those folks never sleep), he was sentenced to life in a high-security prison with a cellmate who snores.

VILLAIN PROFILE: DR DIABOLICAL

With a PhD in evil (as well as PhDs in neuroscience, physics, electrical engineering, and Russian literature), you don't want to risk calling Dr. Natalia Vronksi "Ms." That's DOCTOR Diabolical to you! Few superheroes are up to the challenge of matching wits with this brainy villain—mostly because her bantering includes a lot of *really* big words! When she's not busy assembling bombs or disassembling atoms, Dr. Diabolical enjoys light reading, like *War and Peace*.

24

WHAT KIND OF VILLAIN ARE YOU UP AGAINST?

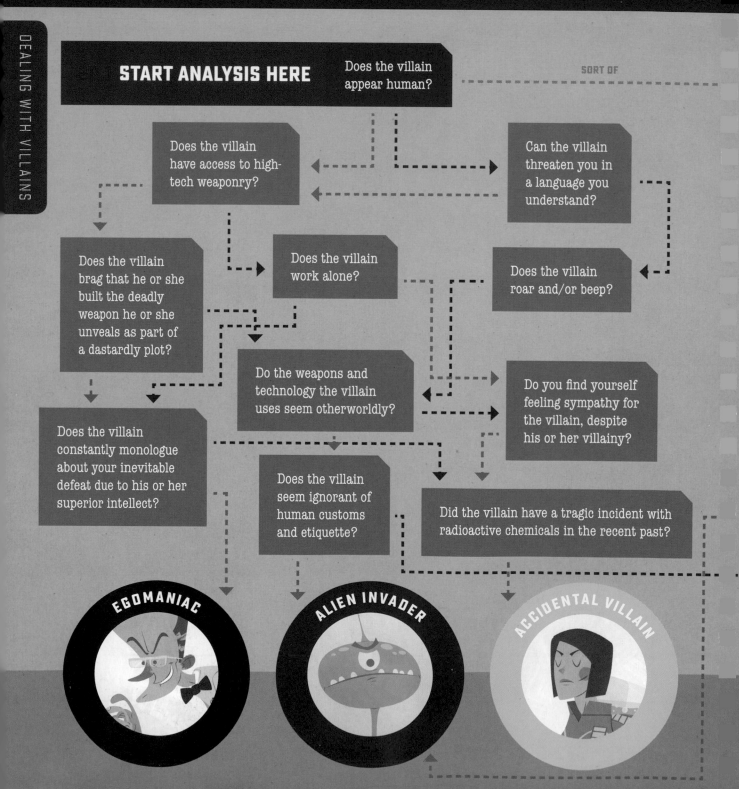

START ANALYSIS HERE Does the villain appear human?

SORT OF

Does the villain have access to high-tech weaponry?

Can the villain threaten you in a language you understand?

Does the villain brag that he or she built the deadly weapon he or she unveals as part of a dastardly plot?

Does the villain work alone?

Does the villain roar and/or beep?

Do the weapons and technology the villain uses seem otherworldly?

Do you find yourself feeling sympathy for the villain, despite his or her villainy?

Does the villain constantly monologue about your inevitable defeat due to his or her superior intellect?

Does the villain seem ignorant of human customs and etiquette?

Did the villain have a tragic incident with radioactive chemicals in the recent past?

EGOMANIAC

ALIEN INVADER

ACCIDENTAL VILLAIN

What equipment should you take? What suit should you wear? Is backup necessary? Before you can answer these questions, you need to ask the most important question of all: WHAT ARE YOU UP AGAINST?

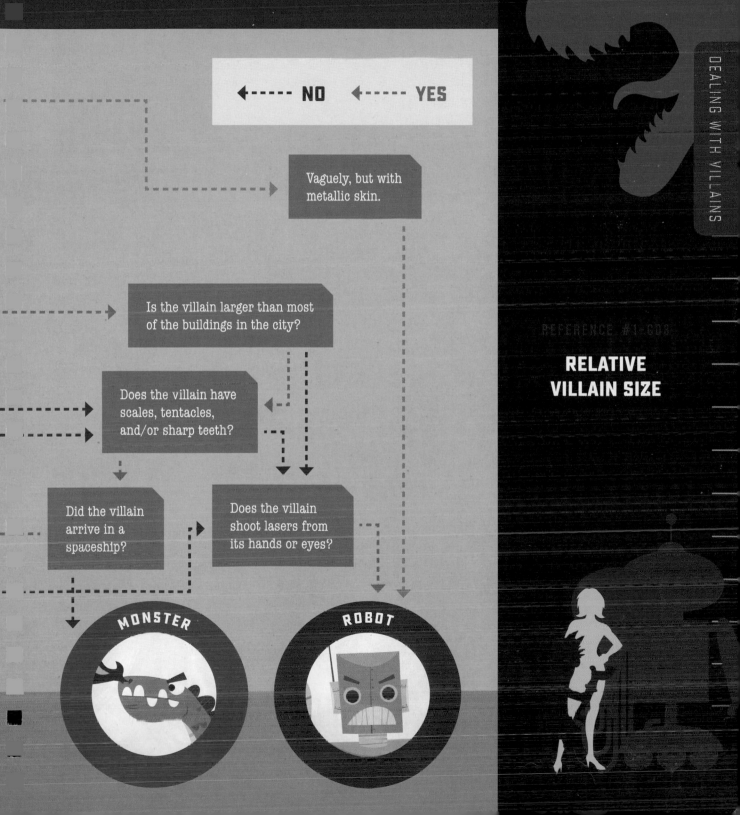

←----- NO ←----- YES

Vaguely, but with metallic skin.

Is the villain larger than most of the buildings in the city?

Does the villain have scales, tentacles, and/or sharp teeth?

Did the villain arrive in a spaceship?

Does the villain shoot lasers from its hands or eyes?

MONSTER

ROBOT

REFERENCE #1-003

RELATIVE VILLAIN SIZE

KNOW YOUR VILLAINS:
2C.1 THE EGOMANIAC

DESCRIPTION	An egomaniac is characterized by a large ego, fueled by a larger inferiority complex, all housed within an even larger cranium. He has usually been scheming world domination plots since childhood. However, his most fiendish plots typically occur in the years clinically called "the midlife crisis," though he prefers superatomic machines of destruction over the usual red sports car.
STRENGTHS	Enormous intellect. Ability to command vast hoards of weaker-minded minions.
WEAKNESSES	Evil plots are usually overcomplicated and thus fraught with holes. Penchant for theatrical flair. Hates getting his clothes dirty.
SUIT	Cashmere sweater and vintage bowtie.
WEAPON	His latest machine of mass destruction.
HENCHMEN	Assorted robots and weak-minded entities of varying degrees of menace.

PUGET SOUND TURNED TO GRAPE JELLY

Seattle—Residents awoke this morning to a sticky situation. Overnight, the entirety of the Puget Sound turned into miles of purple, viscous grape jelly. No one has yet claimed responsibility, but suspicions immediately fell on Butter Nutter, the infamous villain. Nutter escaped from maximum security prison three months ago, where he was serving a life sentence for his attempt to turn Washington DC into a giant peanut butter sandwich. Clean-up is still underway in the nation's capital, and

These types of plots almost always have a melodramatic egomaniac behind them.

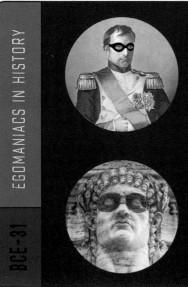

NAPOLEON
Small in stature but unmatched in ego. Achieved great conquest, but was finally defeated by Wonder Wellington in 1815.

GUY FAWKES
Part of a plot to destroy the British government in 1605. The plot was foiled by the authorities, who acted on a tip in an anonymous letter. It is commonly held among supers that the letter was sent by Thames the Mighty.

NERO
Emperor of Rome from 54 to 68 AD. Known for his brutality, he is also blamed by some for the massive fire that destroyed much of Rome in 64 AD. The fire was eventually put out by Aquius Maximus, whom Nero never thanked.

GENGHIS KHAN
Ammassed a giant empire in Asia by the end of his life. The circumstances of his death are still unknown, but supers agree it happened sometime around his fight with Ramen Man.

EGOMANIAC ANATOMY: #564-C

WEAKNESS PROFILE

Usually followed by a hoard of smaller minions. Easy to engage one-on-one, but challenging when facing groups of over 150.

Enormous intellect is a strength, but is often accompanied by a love of theatrics and monologues.

Hates getting his signature cashmere sweater and bowtie dirty.

Latest destruction machine (dramatically attached to the villain himself, of course).

VILLAIN PROFILE: PROFESSOR A

Would have named himself Professor X, but he didn't want anyone else's name coming before his in the alphabet (typical). Professor A made a fortune inventing nuclear weapons, retired early, and now spends his free time on more creative plots (like adding his face to Mount Rushmore).

High-end shoes are trendy, but highly impractical in battle. Consider exploiting.

Weak physical strength (villain prefers to rely on intellect alone).

2C KNOW YOUR VILLAINS:
2C.2 THE ACCIDENTAL VILLAIN

DESCRIPTION	An accidental villain is the most complicated you will face. She is characterized by a conflicted personality, usually the result of a past traumatic accident involving acid, radiation, scary animals, or, in the worst case, radioactive animals made of acid. She is out for revenge on all that is good and right in the world—mostly, that means you.
STRENGTHS	Immense drive and motivation. A tragic backstory that can weaken your resolve.
WEAKNESSES	Debilitating trust issues. Conflicted personality that can lead to momentary indecisiveness (always helpful in tight situations). Strong emotional attachment to pets.
SUIT	Titanium armor.
WEAPON	Mixed use of chemicals, computer viruses, and child psychology.
HENCHMEN	Accidental villains usually work alone. However, they are often seen with a hench-pet.

Accidental villains are elusive and tough to track, but a handy tracking chip on her hench-pet will do the trick.

INFAMOUS ACCIDENTAL VILLAIN HENCH-PETS

Over the years, some hench-pets have become almost as famous as the accidental villains that feed them.

BANDIT

Quick, stealthy, and absolutely silent, Bandit has been implicated in several high-profile bank robberies. His calling card is unmistakable—you might want to take a pooper scooper with you.

MOUSETRAP

A criminal mastermind in her own right, the ingenious Mousetrap can navigate a 6-foot-square maze in under 3 seconds. She is best known for her role in the infamous Gruyère Heist last year.

PETUNIA

Charming and mysterious, Petunia can take on innumerable roles with incredible theatrical precision. Superheroes have spotted her posing as an orphaned girl, a trick-or-treater, a Hollywood extra, and most recently, a tour guide at Fort Knox.

DR. CLAWS

With a fierce attitude and the claws to match, Dr. Claws has terrorized cities and nations for years. He first appeared in villain circles as the hench-pet of The Dogcatcher, the accidental villain known for kidnapping the US president's pet poodle.

ACCIDENTAL VILLAIN ANATOMY: #574-C

WEAKNESS PROFILE

Conflicted personality can lead to indecision.

Tragic backstory makes villain exceptionally prone to emotional monogloues.

Often uses chemical weapons, which can easily backfire if properly sabatoged.

Even the best titanium armor often leaves exposed areas, usually in the joints.

Titanium suit can warm up quickly. Consider luring villain to hot climates for battle.

With the exception of hench-pets, the villain usually works alone (which is nice when you don't feel like battling an army of robots).

VILLAIN PROFILE: CALAMITY BANE

With a zany love of chemicals and things that go BOOM, Calamity Bane has been a formidable enemy for many years. Orphaned at age 7 when a superhero accidentally clipped her parents' car, she has made it her life's work to see that all superheroes go BOOM, too.

Acid burns are an occupational hazard when taking this villain on.

CONSIDER THIS:

Sometimes your greatest weapon against invading aliens is the smallest thing of all: germs.

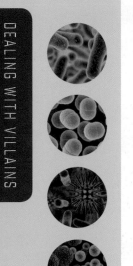

2C KNOW YOUR VILLAINS:
2C.3 THE ALIEN INVADER

DESCRIPTION	The *alien invaders* classification comprises any type of creature that originates from outside the earth's own atmosphere. Oddly enough, they are often humanoid in appearance, though their special abilities (laser breath, advanced technology, and extra tentacles, to name just a few) make them especially tricky foes. Note: If facing an entire invading army, we recommend getting backup—a *lot* of backup.
STRENGTHS	Advanced technology. Surprise arrival.
WEAKNESSES	Little knowledge of humans. Unaccustomed to the peculiarities of earthlife, including earth's atmosphere, invisible germs, and the lure of Internet cat videos.
SUIT	Varies.
WEAPON	Varies, but it's usually better than anything you have.
HENCHMEN	None, though they often have an unassuming human accomplice.

ALIEN INVASION FORMATIONS

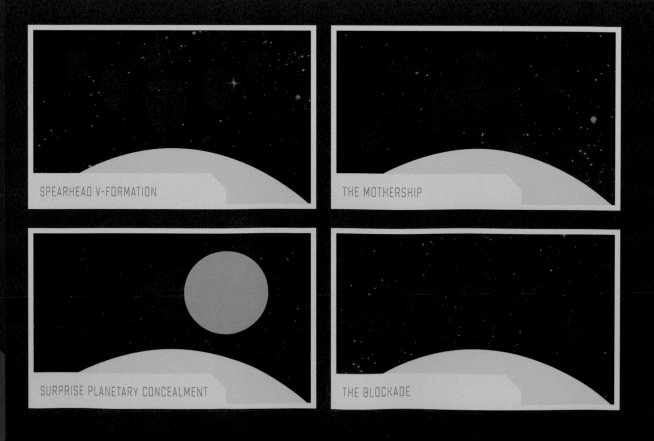

SPEARHEAD V-FORMATION

THE MOTHERSHIP

SURPRISE PLANETARY CONCEALMENT

THE BLOCKADE

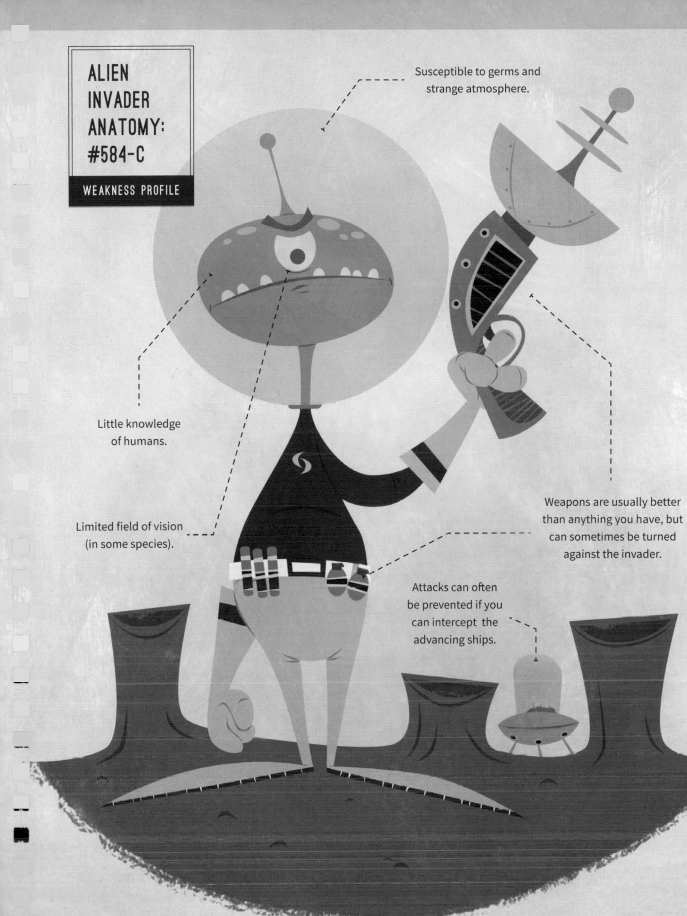

ALIEN INVADER ANATOMY: #584-C

WEAKNESS PROFILE

Susceptible to germs and strange atmosphere.

Little knowledge of humans.

Limited field of vision (in some species).

Weapons are usually better than anything you have, but can sometimes be turned against the invader.

Attacks can often be prevented if you can intercept the advancing ships.

DEALING WITH VILLAINS

KNOW YOUR VILLAINS:
2C.4 THE MONSTER

Flame-proof fabrics are advisable! (see page 72)

DESCRIPTION	The *monster* classification comprises any type of creature that originates from inside the earth's own atmosphere. Unlike alien invaders, monsters are usually *not* humanoid in appearance, and frequently take the form of a mutated animal (lizards and insects are particularly common).
STRENGTHS	Humongous size and strength.
WEAKNESSES	Less intelligent. Often fights alone (but you better stop them before they lay eggs).
SUIT	None, though the super thick hide is usually better than titanium.
WEAPON	None, but their fire breath is enough for you to handle.

Option: You can use packaged mac and cheese, but the homemade variety tastes better!

2C.5 MACARONI MONSTER

Some monsters are actually quite tasty. Eat this one before it eats you!

Your weapon of choice

SUPPLIES:

1 package (16 ounces) macaroni, cooked and drained

1 cup half and half

3/4 cup butter

1 cup freshly grated parmesan cheese

Salt and pepper to taste

1/2 cup frozen peas

1/2 cup frozen corn

Chopped parsley for garnish (optional)

MISSION:

1. Place butter and half and half in a saucepan and heat until the butter melts. Lower heat and stir in the cheese until melted. Stir in peas and corn and season with salt and pepper to taste.

2. Place macaroni in a bowl and pour the sauce over the noodles. Top with chopped parsley. Toss gently and serve.

SERVES 4

Low intelligence levels.

Blind spots for possible approach.

Easily distracted.

MONSTER ANATOMY: #594-C

WEAKNESS PROFILE

Large exposed area not protected by scaly hide.

Make sure the defeated monster didn't hide eggs somewhere, or you'll be fighting this battle again- and it won't be against just one.

EASTER IS EARLY, BUT NOT PRETTY

2C KNOW YOUR VILLAINS:
2C.6 THE ROBOT

DESCRIPTION	Robots are usually the creation of another villain (see *2C.1 The Egomaniac*), but you'll often have to fight one before getting through to the villain himself. Robots come in a variety of sizes and materials, depending on the villain's own creativity and how much free time you've let him have. A typical superhero's career will face everything from robotic butlers (fairly easy to deal with, and they offer complimentary boot shining) to colossal mechanical juggernauts.
STRENGTHS	Advanced artificial intelligence. Multiple weapons systems. Nearly impenetrable armor.
WEAKNESSES	Must work within its programming, which can be manipulated.
SUIT	Depends on material used in construction.
WEAPON	Varies, though common choices are heat-seeking missiles and 360-degree lasers.

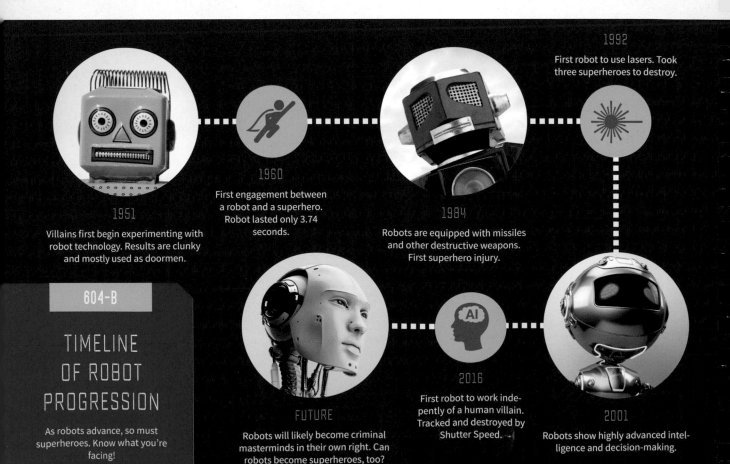

604-B

TIMELINE OF ROBOT PROGRESSION

As robots advance, so must superheroes. Know what you're facing!

1951
Villains first begin experimenting with robot technology. Results are clunky and mostly used as doormen.

1960
First engagement between a robot and a superhero. Robot lasted only 3.74 seconds.

1984
Robots are equipped with missiles and other destructive weapons. First superhero injury.

1992
First robot to use lasers. Took three superheroes to destroy.

FUTURE
Robots will likely become criminal masterminds in their own right. Can robots become superheroes, too?

2016
First robot to work independently of a human villain. Tracked and destroyed by Shutter Speed.

2001
Robots show highly advanced intelligence and decision-making.

Destroy antenna
to disrupt
communications.

Dismember each arm
to disable weapons.

Vulnerable
exposed wiring.

Reprogramming
may be an option if
you're skilled with
computers (and can
get close enough).

Lure heat-seeking
missiles back towards
robot, then duck at the
last second.

May run out of fuel.
Consider evading
until fuel is depleted.

ROBOT
ANATOMY:
#604-C

WEAKNESS PROFILE

2D HOW TO GET A VILLAIN MONOLOGUING

2D.1 SHAKESPEAREAN TRAINING FOR SUPERHEROES

When your back's against the wall and the villain is laughing at your inevitable demise, your surest way out of this sticky situation is getting the villain monologuing. Most villains are, after all, schooled in Shakespearean theatre, and none can pass up the chance to deliver an Oscar-worthy performance. Here are 7 lines that are sure to get the villain babbling while you slip away.

STAGEHAND'S
SUPER IMPROV NIGHT
Master Your One-Liners!

50 CENTS

ADMIT ONE

N° 072614

"TELL ME, HOW LONG HAVE YOU BEEN PLOTTING THIS?"

"IS THIS BECAUSE OF WHAT I DID TO YOU IN JUNIOR HIGH?"

If you need help delivering these lines flawlessly, a couple of nights at Stagehand's Super Improv Night are just the ticket . . . literally.

"YOU'RE A [INSERT YOUR FAVORITE INSULT]."

(NO VILLAIN CAN STAND LETTING YOU HAVE THE LAST WORD, ESPECIALLY IF IT'S AN INSULT. FOR AN EXHAUSTIVE LIST OF VILLAIN INSULT IDEAS, SEE THE NEXT PAGE.)

"IT'S NOT TOO LATE FOR YOU, [INSERT VILLAIN'S CHILDHOOD NAME]. COME OVER TO THE GOOD SIDE!"

"YOU'LL NEVER GET AWAY WITH THIS!"

(OH, THEY CAN'T RESIST THIS ONE!)

"BUT WHY? HOW COULD YOU DO SOMETHING LIKE THIS?"

(WORKS LIKE A CHARM IF DONE WITH JUST ENOUGH OF A DESPERATE WHINE.)

"I'LL NEVER JOIN YOU!"   (MENTIONING THAT YOU'RE A LONG-LOST SON WOULD BE A NICE TOUCH.)

2D.2 STAGEHAND'S

SUPERVILLAIN INSULT GENERATOR

Running low on catchy insults to sling at every new villain in town? Just use this easy insult generator to create thousands of unique, stick-it-to-the-bad-man insults. Simply choose a random word from each of the three columns, put them together, and you'll have a real zinger. For example, tomorrow's villain might be a "Happiness-Destroying Cad" or a "Peace-Disturbing Scumbag." The possibilities are endless! (Well, technically there are 5,832 possible combinations, but who's counting?)

A		B		C
Justice		Destroying		Fiend
Peace		Hating		Scoundrel
Happiness		Disrupting		Rascal
American Way		Crashing		Cad
Tranquility		Warping		Menace
Freedom		Demolishing		Villain
Joy		Defying		Rat
Safety		Wrecking		Dog
Balance		Ruining		Miscreant
Order		Spoiling		Felon
Harmony		Crushing		Charlatan
Integrity		Shattering		Rogue
Truth		Harming		Crook
Security		Zapping		Scumbag
Law		Disturbing		Con
Honor		Wasting		Lowlife
Trust		Flouting		Ruffian
Hope		Mocking		Knave

Stagehand is a Vegas showman by day and superhero crime fighter by night. A graduate of the Juilliard School, his clever theatrics and acrobatics leave crowds crying with laughter and villains chasing their tails. A master of one-liners and monologue baiting, Stagehand has since started regular improv nights to help fellow supers hone their own skills.

2E DEALING WITH A WORLD DOMINATION PLOT

World domination plots vary in their intensity and dramatic flair, but all will require quick thinking to stop. Skilled superheroes can thwart up to three plots at a time (with breaks for lunch, tea, and dinner, of course).

ARIZONA, USA 7:19 PM
A bizarre attempt to fill the Grand Canyon with nacho cheese. Villain remains unknown, but bring plenty of backup . . . and chips.

2E.1 HOW TO SPOT A WORLD DOMINATION PLOT

No one liked the boy who cried wolf, and no one trusts a superhero who shouts "Intergalactic plot to dominate the world!" too often, either. Before you sound the alarm and raise everyone's blood pressure, quickly run through the following exercise.

Does the emerging plot:

☐ Involve strategic attacks on Washington DC, New York City, and, for some strange reason, Mount Rushmore?

☐ Have at least 3 obvious loopholes that high-ranking officials have ignored?

☐ Involve a supervillain of such evil repute that he has his own musical score?

☐ Include nuclear superbombs, android armies, and/or the invasion of an alien species from another dimension?

☐ Make you want to call in sick?

If you checked 4 or more of the above statements, congratulations! You have a Level 5 world domination plot on your hands. Good luck—you're going to need it.

PACIFIC OCEAN

ATLANTIC OCEAN

LIMA, PERU 3:19 PM
A monster attack on the Presidential Palace. Monster's motives remain unclear, but probably include destruction, general mayhem, and government control. Or maybe it's just hungry. Really, really hungry.

STONEHENGE, BRITAIN 4:14 AM

A nuclear missile launch from under Stonehenge. Must intercept within 15 minutes. UPDATE: Must intercept within 10 minutes. UPDATE: Must intercept within 5 minutes. UPDATE: IS ANYBODY EVEN READING THIS?

GREAT WALL, CHINA 11:23 PM

The Great Wall of China has been electrified and appears to be part of a continent-wide electric circut. Impending alien invasion suspected.

PACIFIC OCEAN 1:03 PM

A massive tsunami from an artificial earthquake beneath the ocean floor. Suspected villain: Seismograph. Areas in danger: well, the entire world.

ARCTIC
OCEAN

PACIFIC
OCEAN

INDIAN
OCEAN

MAP KEY

😫 Act of insanity

🔌 Technological mayhem

☁ Intended world destruction

🏛 Government takeover

TODAY'S EVIL PLOTS

0 5 AND COUNTING . . .

2F VILLAIN WEAPONS:

Villain weapons are as versatile as the crazy personalities behind them. From freeze rays to things that go BOOM, it's best to have a sound knowledge of the destructive possibilities. On the following pages, you'll find helpful suggestions (and some delicious mockups) for handling some of the more common weapons you might face.

2F.1 WEAPON CLASSES

CLASS A	An existential threat with a magnitude capable of destroying an entire planet.
CLASS B	A catastrophic threat. Is capable of destroying a large city or small country.
CLASS C	A major threat, but poses a risk only to an isolated area. Best tackled in groups.
CLASS D	A significant threat, but can only attack one individual at a time.
CLASS E	Minor annoyance, but worth a good laugh.

HISTORIC EXAMPLES

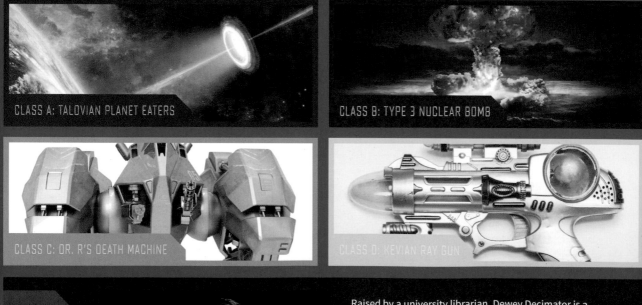

CLASS A: TALOVIAN PLANET EATERS

CLASS B: TYPE 3 NUCLEAR BOMB

CLASS C: DR. R'S DEATH MACHINE

CLASS D: KEVIAN RAY GUN

Raised by a university librarian, Dewey Decimator is a stickler for accuracy and organization. Apart from his defeat of Colonel Clutter in 1987, Dewey Decimator's biggest contribution to superherodom is his systematic categorization of villains and their weapons. He also classified types of pigeons, woodland mushrooms, and chewing gum, but this is considered slightly less helpful to the cause. When not fighting supervillains, Dewey can be found straightening his collection of Norwegian paperclips.

2F.2 VILLAIN WEAPONS THAT DIDN'T GET PAST THE DRAWING BOARD

Some weapons just aren't meant to see the light of day. While it's unlikely you'll face these in real life, these weapon plans—recovered by a squad of superheroes—reveal what fiendish things villains are capable of. The point? Always expect the unexpected.

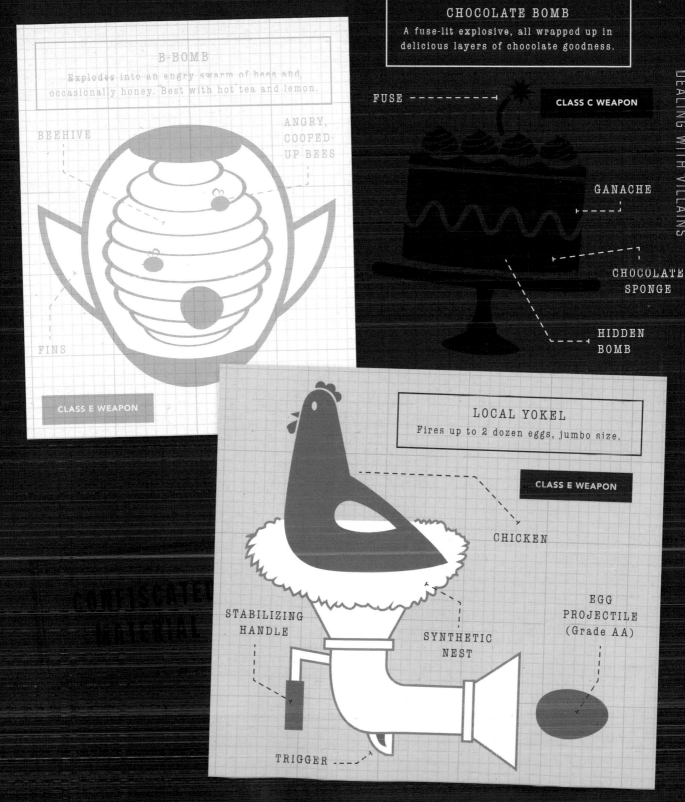

B-BOMB
Explodes into an angry swarm of bees and occasionally honey. Best with hot tea and lemon.

BEEHIVE

ANGRY, COOPED-UP BEES

FINS

CLASS E WEAPON

CHOCOLATE BOMB
A fuse-lit explosive, all wrapped up in delicious layers of chocolate goodness.

FUSE

CLASS C WEAPON

GANACHE

CHOCOLATE SPONGE

HIDDEN BOMB

LOCAL YOKEL
Fires up to 2 dozen eggs, jumbo size.

CLASS E WEAPON

CHICKEN

STABILIZING HANDLE

SYNTHETIC NEST

EGG PROJECTILE (Grade AA)

TRIGGER

CONFISCATED MATERIAL

BEATING VILLAIN WEAPONS:
2G.1 THE FREEZE RAY

Cold and sinister, the freeze ray is a standard villain weapon used in most countries. The banana pop version pictured here is absolutely delicious, but stay away from the real thing if you don't want to be shelved in the frozen foods aisle.

FREEZE CHAMBER

COOLING COILS

NOZZLE

COOLANT CELLS

HANDLE

TRIGGER

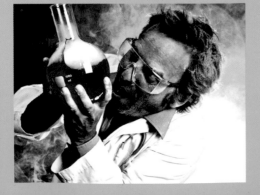

Once an entrepreneur with a billion-dollar ice cream business, Dr. Freeze entered the crime world after his pet poodle got sick from eating five gallons of Superhero Crunch (short fuse, this guy). His first evil venture was turning the Eiffel Tower into a giant fudgsicle. It took authorities three weeks to clean up the mess, and almost as long for French kids to recover from their stomachaches. Since then, Dr. Freeze has attempted to freeze the English Channel, turn Niagra Falls into the world's biggest cherry-flavored slushie, and make ice skating the national pastime of, well, everywhere. His favorite hobby is freezing superheroes, and right now that means YOU.

2G.2 FREEZE RAY BANANA POPS

SUPPLIES:

12 bananas, peeled

12 craft or popsicle sticks

1 package (12 ounces) blue Wilton Candy Melts

12 pieces of black fondant, formed into 1-inch squares, toothpick inserted halfway into each

1 apple, cut into 12 slices, each slice cut in half

Silver, blue, white, and purple sprinkles

1 bag Gummy Lifesavers

Jelly beans

1 package Sour Punch Straws, cut into 2-inch lengths (48 total)

6 large, seedless grapes, cut in half

Mentos

MISSION:

PREPARE THE FROZEN BANANAS

1 Insert the popsicle sticks into the base of the bananas, leaving 2 inches exposed. Wrap the bananas in foil and freeze 8 hours or longer.

2 When ready to assemble, melt Candy Melts in a microwave-safe bowl according to package directions. You may occasionally need to reheat the candy coating during the assembly process.

3 Remove bananas from freezer and unwrap. Place frozen bananas on a foil-lined cookie sheet.

ASSEMBLE THE FREEZE RAYS

1 Form an assembly line of twelve frozen bananas on prepared cookie sheet. After each step, return bananas to the cookie sheet to allow the candy coating to harden; this only takes a minute because the bananas are frozen.

2 Coat each banana completely in the melted candy coating and immediately insert the exposed toothpick end of the black fondant square into the underside center of the banana "gun" to serve as the handle.

3 Dip 1/2 apple slice into the candy coating and insert and attach to the underside of the banana as the trigger.

4 Dip the front-end tip end of each banana into the candy coating and immediately dip into silver sprinkles to create the freeze chamber.

5 Dip a Gummy Lifesaver into the candy coating and attach to the front of each banana, allowing a few minutes to harden before dipping the tip of a blue jelly bean into the candy coating and placing it in the center of the Lifesaver. These will serve as the nozzle.

6 Dip and completely cover three 2-inch strings of Sour Punch Straws in the candy coating. Attach to the gun to create the cooling coils.

7   Dip both end tips of the remaining Sour Punch Straws in the candy coating and attach to the top of the gun to create a horseshoe-shaped cooling coil.

8   Dip a grape half into melted candy coating and attach to the back end of the gun. Immediately dip into a mixture of blue, white, and purple sprinkles for coolant cells.

9   Embellish the gun by adhering jelly beans and Mentos for buttons and lights with a dab of candy coating.

10   Place in freezer uncovered until ready to serve.

MAKES 12

IF YOU DO GET FROZEN . . .

Freeze rays usually aren't lethal, but if you don't want to look like this guy here, it's best to avoid them. In some cases, laser vision can help speed up the melting process. If not, settle in for a long winter—we'll let you know when spring comes.

BEATING VILLAIN WEAPONS:
2G.3 KRYPTONITE

Kryptonite can be lethal in the wrong hands. If you happen to be susceptible to it, stay FAR away. But do try one of these amazing glow-in-the-dark Kryptonite Cupcakes—they're far better than the real thing!

CLEVER WAYS VILLAINS TRY TO HIDE KRYPTONITE

When villains find out your weakness, they will go to great lengths to make sure they use it against you. For superheroes affected by kryptonite, this is especially true. Here are just a few common ruses that villains might use to weaken you on the sly.

1 Fashioning the kryptonite into a ring

2 Blending it into your Lime-Green Energy Smoothie (see page 126 for non kryptonite recipe)

3 Wrapping the kryptonite like a present with colored paper and a bow

4 Tucking the kryptonite inside a fortune cookie ("There is danger in your future.")

26.4 GLOW-IN-THE-DARK KRYPTONITE CUPCAKES

Not everyone is vulnerable to the green menace—in fact, very few are—but kryptonite's unparalleled celebrity status in the world of supers makes these sweet glow-in-the-dark replicas nearly irresistible.

SUPPLIES:

CUPCAKES

1 package yellow or golden cake mix

1 package (8 ounces) cream cheese, room temperature

1/2 cup granulated sugar

1/2 cup water

4 large eggs

1 tablespoon vanilla

1 cup M&M's

FROSTING

1 stick butter, room temperature

1/2 teaspoon almond extract

5 tablespoons tonic water

4 cups powdered sugar

Food coloring

1 package (3 ounces) Jell-O

1 cup boiling water

1 cup chilled tonic water

MISSION:

MAKING THE CUPCAKES

1 Preheat oven to 350 degrees. Line twenty-four cupcake cups with paper liners. Set aside until ready to use.

2 Place all ingredients in a large mixing bowl and beat for 2 minutes until smooth and thickened.

3 Spoon about 1/4 cup batter into each muffin cup and top with 5 to 6 M&M's. Bake about 25 to 30 minutes or until light golden brown.

4 Cool 15 to 30 minutes before frosting.

FROSTING THE CUPCAKES

5 Mix butter until fluffy. Sir in almond extract, 5 tablespoons tonic water, powdered sugar, and a pinch of salt. Mix on low speed until combined. Increase speed and beat for 1 to 2 minutes longer until mixture is fluffy. Add food coloring and mix again to blend color.

6 Frost Glow-in-the-Dark Kryptonite Cupcakes and place in freezer overnight or at least 8 hours.

7 Place Jell-O in a heat safe bowl and add 1 cup boiling water. Whisk to combine. Add 1 cup chilled tonic water and whisk until all Jell-O is dissolved.

8 Pop Jell-O in the fridge to quick chill for 5 to 7 minutes.

9 Remove cupcakes from freezer three at a time, dip into Jell-O, and place back in freezer until all have been dipped.

10 Repeat this process four to six times and allow the cupcakes to chill in fridge at least 30 minutes before serving them under a black light to capture the villainous glow.

MAKES 24 CUPCAKES

DIP CUPCAKES IN JELL-O MIXTURE

USE A BLACK LIGHT TO WATCH THEM GLOW!

WHAT TO DO AGAINST KRYPTONITE

Hopefully it doesn't affect you, but if it does, here are 4 defenses.

Run before it's too close

Melt it with acid

Block it with lead

Call the villain names (not recommended)

BEATING VILLAIN WEAPONS:
2G.5 MIND CONTROL

Mind control is no joke, so if you are going up against a villain with mind control capabilities, it is best to be prepared. Craft your own mind control–prevention helmet to protect your mind and, consequently, the world.

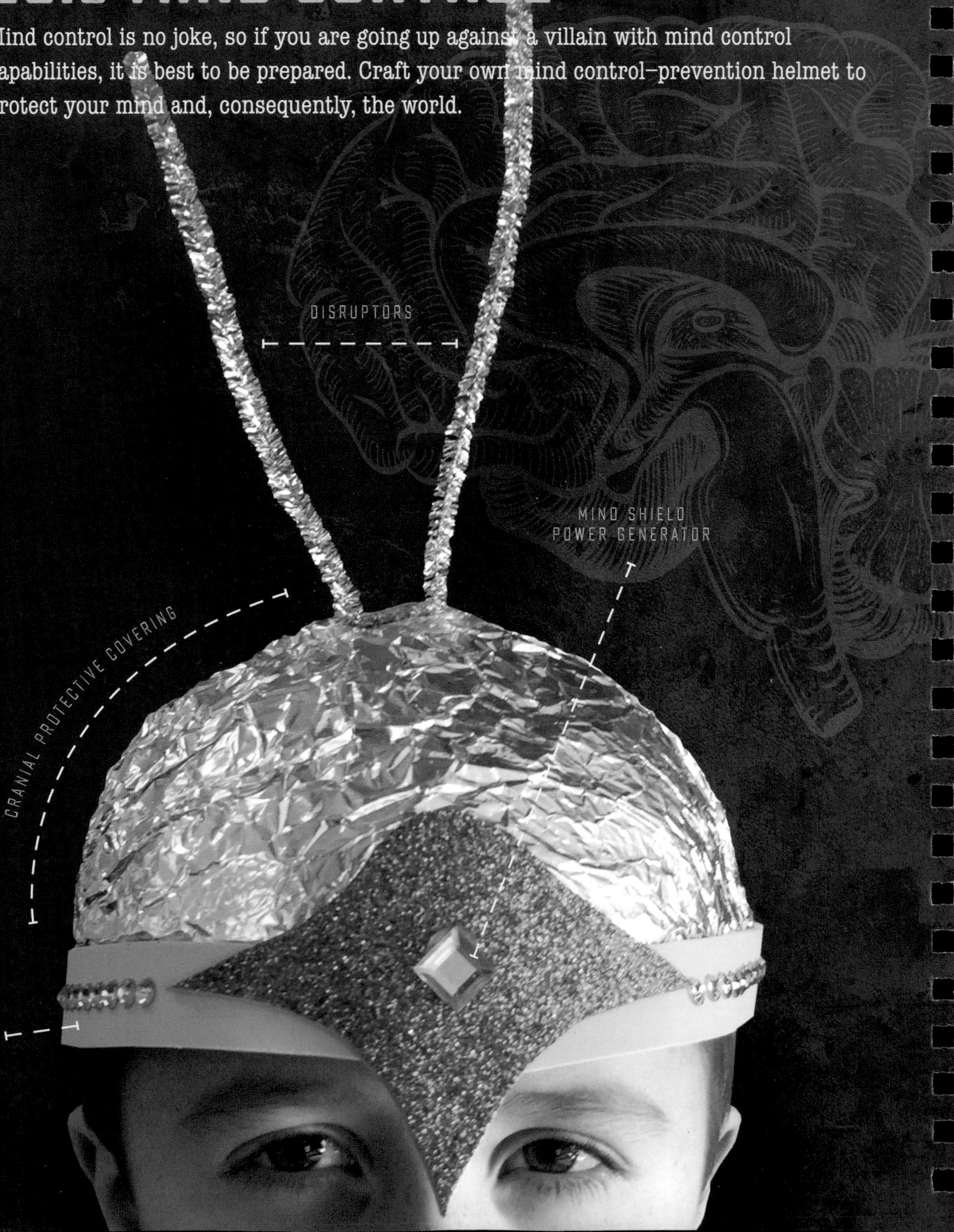

DISRUPTORS

MIND SHIELD
POWER GENERATOR

CRANIAL PROTECTIVE COVERING

FRONTAL
LOBE
OVERLOAD
BUFFER

2G.6 MAKE YOUR OWN MIND CONTROL-PREVENTION HELMET

SUPPLIES:

Aluminum foil

Assorted decorations (pipe cleaners, foam shapes, etc.)

MISSION:

1 Tear or cut a piece of foil into a square (approximately 12 x 12 inches).

2 Place the foil on your head (or the head of the intended superhero), holding it in place at the crown of the head with one hand.

3 Using the other hand, wrap the corners clockwise around your head so they overlap. Slightly roll up the bottom edge to secure the corners in place.

4 Decorate your helmet with the necessary apparatus (pipe cleaners as antennae, etc.) and wear whenever you face a villain with mind control powers.

THE PERILS OF MIND CONTROL

Many supervillains are experts at mind control. If you haven't had time to build your Mind Control–Prevention Helmet, you need to be prepared for what might happen in the event that a villain takes over your mind. It's very possible that the supervillain will force you to:

1 Commit a crime. (Many villains have been known to "persuade" superheroes to rob banks, steal government missiles, or deface public property.)

2 Do the Hokey-Pokey. (You'll put your right hand in. You'll put your right hand out. And you won't be able to do anything about it.)

3 Wear socks with sandals. (Now that's just embarrassing!)

4 Bake a perfect soufflé. (It's much harder than you think.)

5 Babysit his or her children. (It's so hard to find good help these days.)

BEATING VILLAIN WEAPONS:

2G.2 BLACK SLIME

Sticky and menacing, black slime is a weapon with a mind of its own. Because of its tendency to ignore its creator's bidding and work towards its own ambitious ends, black slime is only deployed by villains in times of great need. Its effects on superheroes can be quite potent, but they usually aren't permanent if treated immediately.

ENCYCLOPEDIA SUPERNICUS
137

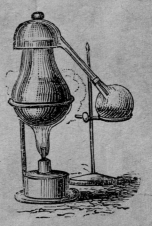

until the superhero was immobilized and the villain escaped.

BLACK SLIME
Tenebris slyk

More commonly known as "black slime," *tenebris slyk* is a gelatinous, sludge-like substance typically found in toxic waste disposal plants or high-security laboratories. Often the by-product of unstable nuclear fusion, varieties of black slime are radioactive and some can take on a life of their own. Once the slime has bonded to a surface, including rubber shoe soles, skin, and polyester—it is virtually impossible to remove.

Researchers have not yet been able to determine whether black slime occurs in nature, but it first made its appearance in scientific circles in 1919, in the laboratory of Dr. Francine Fleusheimer. Her research was instrumental in learning about the properties of black slime—that is, until the slime became sentient, escaped from its containment beaker, and consumed Dr. Fleusheimer and her assistant, Ted. Luckily, their notes were left in-

26.8 TRAINING-GRADE BLACK SLIME

SUPPLIES:

1 cup Elmer's Glue

1 cup warm water

Black paste food coloring (though you can use a different color if you wish)

1/2 cup warm water

1 teaspoon borax

1 teaspoon silver craft glitter

MISSION:

1 Combine glue, 1 cup warm water, and food coloring in a bowl and mix well.

2 In another bowl, combine 1/2 cup warm water with borax. Mix well.

3 Pour the borax water into the glue water and stir with a spoon until it creates slime. Mix in glitter.

4 Store in a covered container for up to two weeks.

Every super knows better than to make real black slime. This stuff is a great alternative you can use during training exercises.

MAKES APPROXIMATELY 2 CUPS

WHAT TO DO AGAINST BLACK SLIME

Once black slime has bonded to a surface, it is nearly impossible to remove (see *Encyclopedia Supernicus*, 137). It's best to dispense of it before it has the opportunity to bond, for which you have several effective options:

LURE IT INTO THE SUN

BLAST IT TO OUTER SPACE

TRAP IT

EAT IT (NOT RECOMMENDED)

If you or another superhero has become bonded to the black slime, don't panic! Lots of soap, scrubbing, and psychotherapy should do the trick.

BEATING VILLAIN WEAPONS:
26.9 BOMBS AND EXPLOSIONS

There isn't a villain on earth who can resist the thrill of explosions. Bombs, missiles, torpedoes, grenades—all in a day's work for today's full-time superheroes.

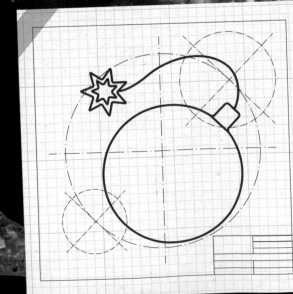

DEALING WITH BOMBS

With the right technical skills, many bombs can be defused. However, most superheroes opt to dispose of bombs the old-fashioned way: throwing them into space, dropping them in the middle of the ocean, or slipping them back into the villain's getaway car.

2G.10 DYNAMITE CANDY BITES

Pop Rocks candy adds a delightful BANG to each piece of these Dynamite Candy Bites. They're the perfect snack to munch on while trying to defuse the real thing. Just keep your eye on that timer!

SUPPLIES:

1 cup crispy rice cereal

1 pound red vanilla candy coating wafers

3 packages Pop Rocks

MISSION:

1 Line a large baking sheet with parchment paper and set aside.

2 Put cereal in a medium bowl and use your hands to crush three or four times; set aside.

3 Microwave vanilla candy coating in a medium heatproof bowl on high for 30 seconds. Stir well and repeat two or three more times, until completely smooth.

4 Stir in cereal. Transfer to prepared baking sheet and spread into a 10x12-inch rectangle. Sprinkle with Pop Rocks. Chill until completely firm (about 30 minutes). Break into pieces and serve.

SERVES 10-12

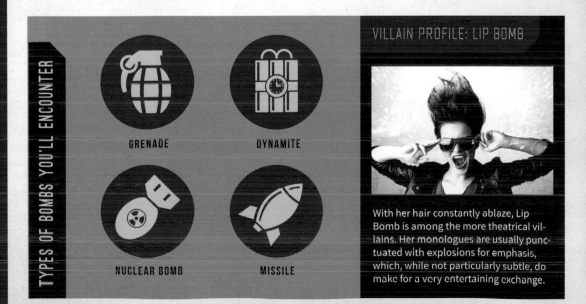

TYPES OF BOMBS YOU'LL ENCOUNTER

GRENADE

DYNAMITE

NUCLEAR BOMB

MISSILE

VILLAIN PROFILE: LIP BOMB

With her hair constantly ablaze, Lip Bomb is among the more theatrical villains. Her monologues are usually punctuated with explosions for emphasis, which, while not particularly subtle, do make for a very entertaining exchange.

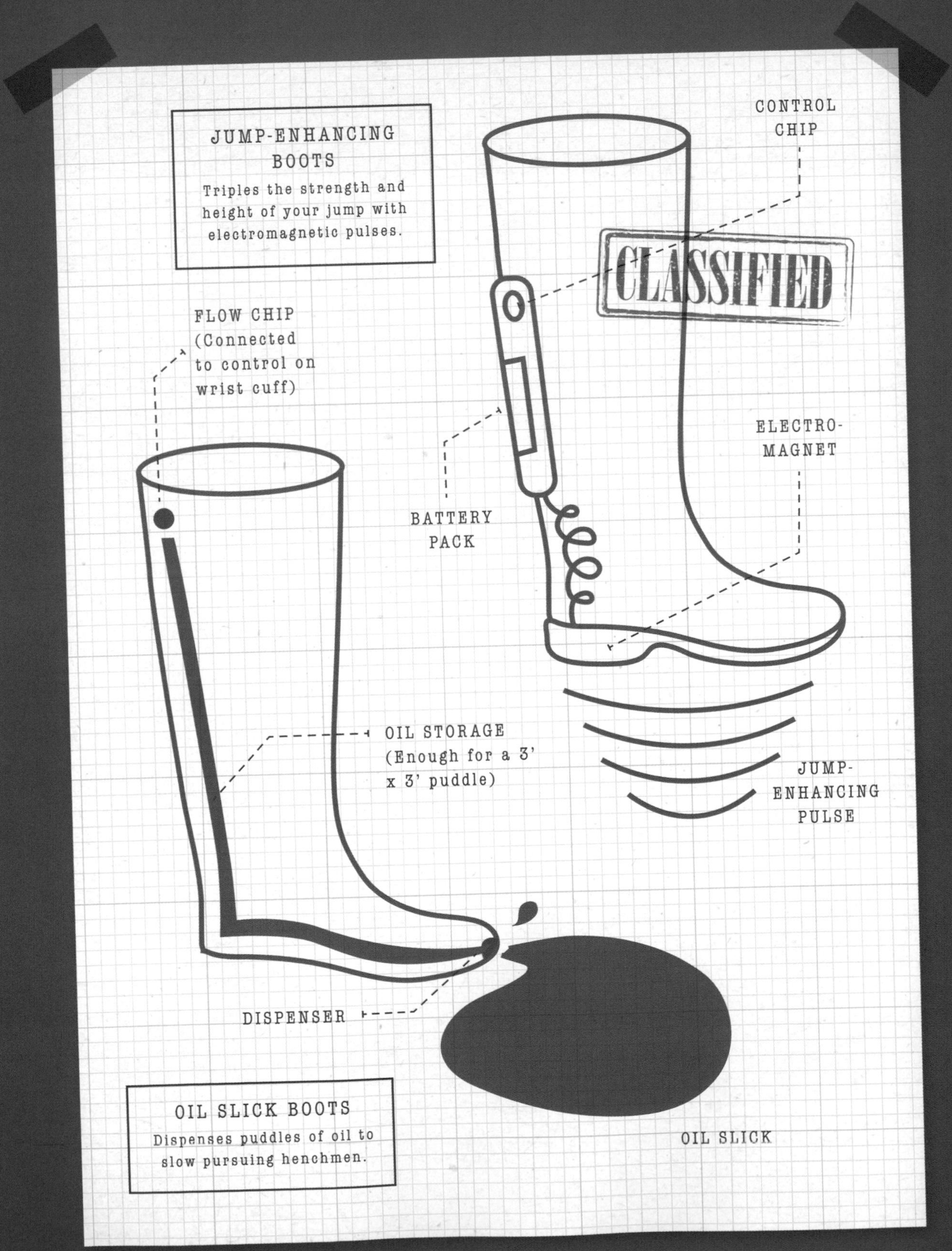

JUMP-ENHANCING BOOTS
Triples the strength and height of your jump with electromagnetic pulses.

CONTROL CHIP

CLASSIFIED

FLOW CHIP
(Connected to control on wrist cuff)

ELECTRO-MAGNET

BATTERY PACK

OIL STORAGE
(Enough for a 3' x 3' puddle)

JUMP-ENHANCING PULSE

DISPENSER

OIL SLICK BOOTS
Dispenses puddles of oil to slow pursuing henchmen.

OIL SLICK

3

GEAR & GADGETS

3A YOUR SUPERSUIT

Creating the perfect supersuit takes a good deal of planning. What colors look best on you? What fabrics best complement your powers? Consider all your options, then roll up your sleeves and get to work.

MASK SEE PAGE 14

Your mask is the only thing protecting your identity, so make sure it's designed well and securely fastened.

THE CAPE SEE PAGE 74

The cape is a traditional part of the superhero's outfit but is now mostly reserved for formal occasions.

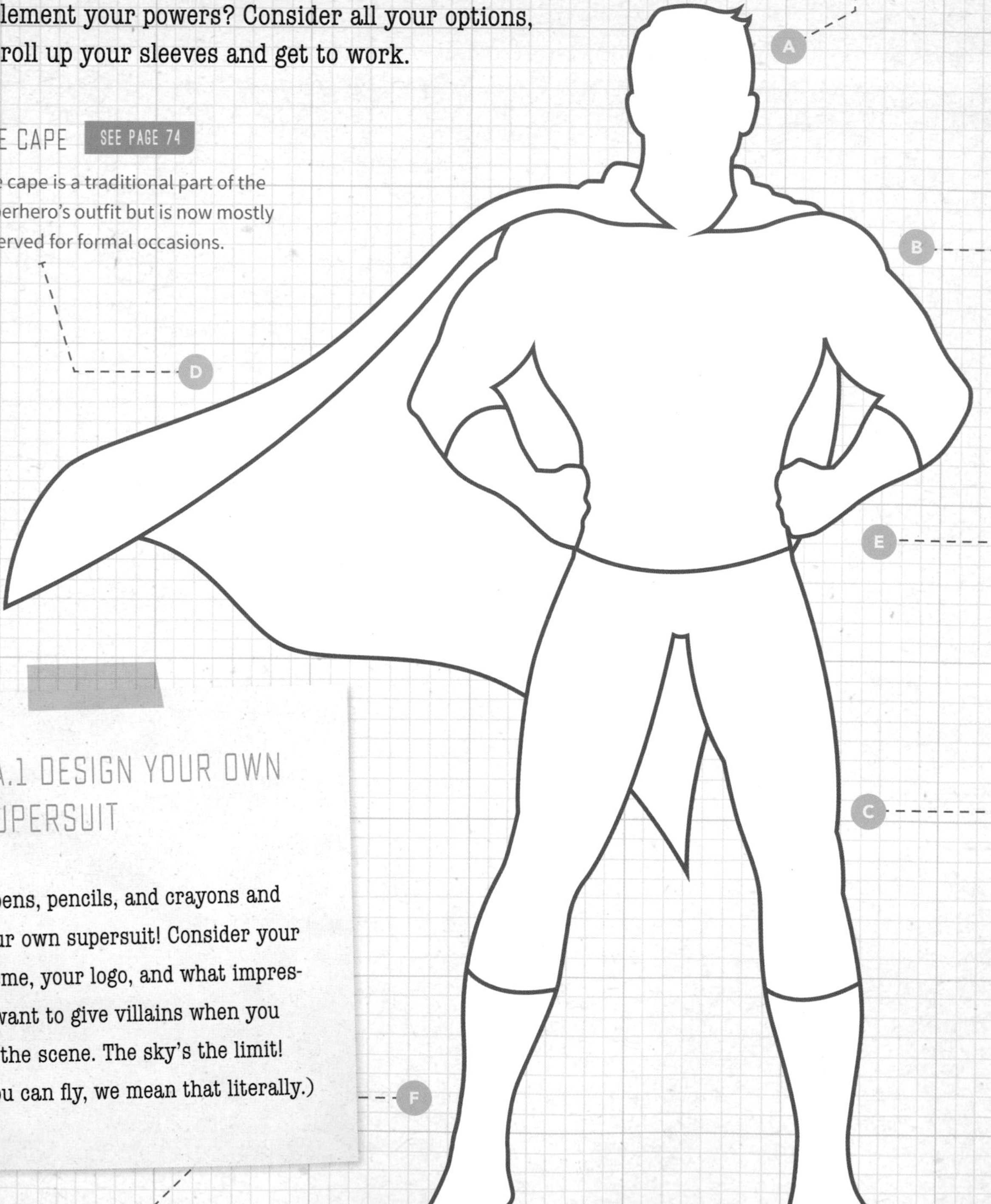

3A.1 DESIGN YOUR OWN SUPERSUIT

Get your pens, pencils, and crayons and design your own supersuit! Consider your color scheme, your logo, and what impression you want to give villains when you arrive on the scene. The sky's the limit! (And if you can fly, we mean that literally.)

BOOTS

If you're planning on tromping through slime, mud, or collapsed buildings, you'll want strong boots that hold up well under heavy use. No flip-flops, please.

CC FROM THE FILES OF
CHRISTOPHER CARDALL
FOUNDER, SUPERHERO DESIGNER FASHION

SHIRT

Your everyday shirt should breathe well, but should also protect you from minor lasers, bullets, and teeth. Battles with more advanced foes may require additional armor.

YOUR LOGO SEE PAGE 131

Your logo is your calling card, so be sure to make it large and visible. You don't want your nemesis to need glasses to see when you've arrived.

TOO SMALL   **TOO UNEVEN**   **JUST RIGHT**

TEXTILE SELECECTION

45B-1

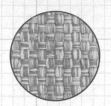 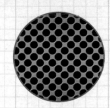

TRADITIONAL
Simple, lightweight, and appropriate for everyday super operations.

ARMORED LAYER
A good choice when facing heavily armed foes or invading armies.

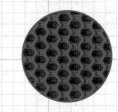 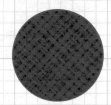

MESH
Breathes great. Excellent for hand-to-hand combat.

FLAME RETARDANT
A must-have when facing monsters or pyros.

GLOVES & WRIST CUFFS SEE PAGE 77

Gloves and wrist cuffs are a must for sifting through rubble, channeling lava, and hand-to-hand combat.

LEGGINGS

If you don't want to be patching holes every night, you'll need your leggings to be made of a material that can withstand lots of running, jumping, and kicking.

SUPERSUIT COLOR SCHEMES

Nothing says "I'm here to save the day" like the bold colors of a dynamite supersuit. But choose your colors wisely—you don't want to look like you just robbed a pajama store.

Fab Fifties

Nightfall

Fireball

Sugar and Spice But Not So Nice

American Classic

THE CAPE QUESTION

While they usually aren't practical for battle, capes are a staple in the traditional superhero wardrobe and a must for public appearances. The easy T-Shirt Cape below will make pleasing your fans a cinch.

WHEN TO WEAR YOUR CAPE

1 **Formal events:** Galas, fundraisers, awards ceremonies, and weddings all warrant formal superwear—that means a cape (and possibly a tie).

2 **Photoshoots:** Strike a pose with your cape and you'll cut a much more impressive figure.

3 **Cold weather:** In a pinch, your cape can double as a coat or blanket.

4 **Fan club meet-and-greets:** Give the people what they want.

WHEN *NOT* TO WEAR YOUR CAPE

1 **While battling a monster:** You'll only give him another way to catch you.

2 **When flying long distances:** Though it might look dashing, a cape creates far too much drag.

3 **While in disguise:** Your cape will give you away quicker than you can say, "No really, guys, I'm going to a costume party!"

 ## 38.1 MAKE YOUR OWN T-SHIRT CAPE

SUPPLIES:

Large t-shirt (used or pre-washed)

Scissors

Heat transfer vinyl, in 1–3 colors (some retailers even carry metallic-looking vinyl)

MISSION:

1 Turn the t-shirt inside out so you can see the seams. Cut off the sleeves.

2 Cut along the side seams of the shirt all the way up. Leave the entire ribbed neck intact.

 OPTIONAL: Angle the line of your cut in toward the center slightly so the bottom of the cape is wider than the top.

3 With the sides cut, open the t-shirt so both sides lay flat. Following the curve of the neckline, cut off the front of the t-shirt, beginning at one shoulder seam and curving around the ribbed neck to meet the line back at the other shoulder.

TIP: Be sure the line of the cape smoothly transitions into the arch of the neckline, no matter the width of the arch.

4 Clear away extra material. Cape should lay flat with neckline ribbing intact. Trim the length of the cape to fit your super's size.

5 Design and create your logo on heat transfer vinyl.

6 Place the cape on a hard, flat surface that will not be affected by the heat of an iron. Using the heat transfer vinyl, cut out your super logo or another creative design to decorate the cape. IMPORTANT: Many heat transfer papers require you to cut out your design in reverse. If your logo includes any letters, check the manufacturer's instructions, and if this is the case, be sure to cut them out backward so they will transfer correctly.

7 Follow the manufacturer's instructions for applying the vinyl and peeling back the plastic, and use caution with the hot iron. Be sure to iron all the edges and corners well to make sure your design sticks completely.

8 Allow all decorations to cool completely before donning the cape.

TIP: You can layer two or more colors of vinyl to create different patterns. Just apply the layers one at a time and allow each one to cool at least 45 seconds before applying another layer.

OPTIONAL: You can also buy plain heat transfer paper, create a logo on your computer, flip it to mirror image, print it, and transfer it to the cape.

HOW TO CUT THE T-SHIRT

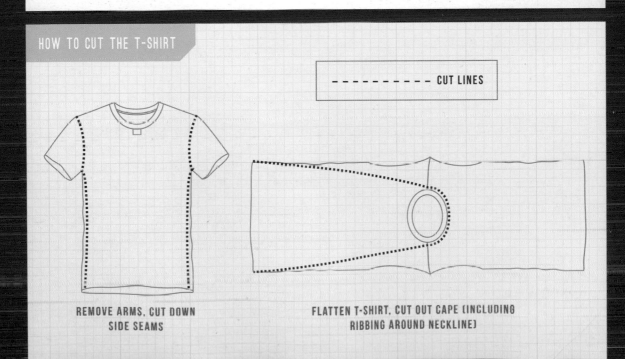

– – – – – – – – – – CUT LINES

REMOVE ARMS, CUT DOWN
SIDE SEAMS

FLATTEN T-SHIRT, CUT OUT CAPE (INCLUDING
RIBBING AROUND NECKLINE)

ACCESSORIES

A few well-placed accessories can go a long way in enhancing your image. Many busy superheroes order these from specialty catalogs (see below), but these services are now largely defunct. It's just as well—no one liked showing up at a party wearing the same outfit as someone else.

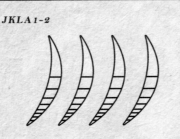

3C.1 MAKE YOUR OWN WRIST CUFFS

Every supersuit needs a pair of wrist cuffs. These might be functional or purely ornamental, but either way, they are sure to perfect your superhero look.

SUPPLIES:

Cardboard toilet paper rolls (or paper towel rolls, if you want your cuffs to be a little longer)

Scissors

Construction paper (bold colors work best)

Craft glue

Markers, paper decals, or other decorations

Assorted buttons

MISSION:

1   Cut the paper roll in half lengthwise. Flex it a bit, without creating a crease, to be sure the cuff will easily fit on the hero's wrist.

2   Cut a piece of construction paper to completely cover the cuff. Secure the paper with glue and allow to dry for 5 minutes.

3   When the glue is reasonably dry, decorate the cuff with your super logo or color scheme using markers, shapes cut from the construction paper, or any other decals you think will help you vanquish evil in style.

4   If you want to make your cuffs fashionable *and* functional, use glue to add a power or booster button. Be sure to let the glue dry completely (at least 30 minutes) before wearing the cuffs into battle.

WRIST CUFFS RISE IN POPULARITY

March 31—Supers are embracing wrist cuffs in droves. Super Emporium, the leading superhero outfitter, has reported that wrist cuff sales have increased by nearly 46% over last year. The increase in demand is largely the

3C.2 MAKE YOUR OWN GLOVES

SUPPLIES:

1 pair of gloves

2 pieces of felt, cut in shapes shown below

Needle and thread to match the color of felt and gloves

MISSION:

1 Sew the felt cutouts to the gloves, lining up the edge of the felt with the little finger of the glove. Make sure the part of the felt that goes around the wrist of the glove is a little loose to allow for stretching and pulling when conquering villains.

2 Sew the edges of the felt together.

3 Repeat on the other glove.

4 Decorate as desired.

GEAR & GADGETS

SHAPES

1 PAIR OF GLOVES

SMALL CURVE OF FELT SHOULD BE THE SAME LENGTH AS CIRCUMFRENCE OF GLOVE'S OPENING

FELT PIECE #1

FELT PIECE #2

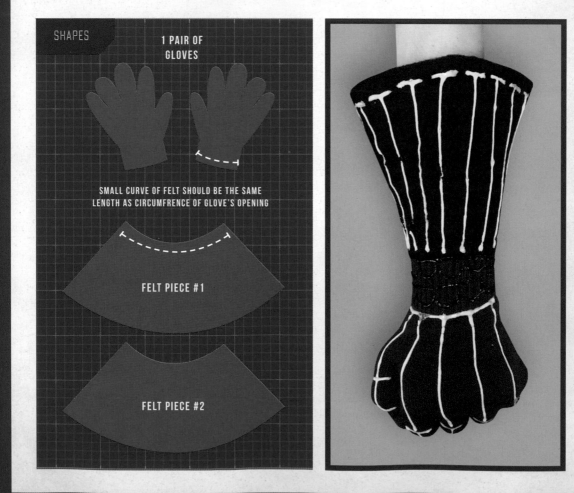

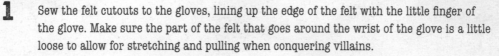

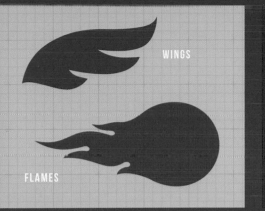

WINGS

FLAMES

SUPERSHOES, AWAAAAAAAY!

3C.3 MAKE YOUR OWN SUPERSHOES

Superheroes have to travel quickly to save the day! To give you extra speed, transform your ordinary shoes into super shoes with wings and flames.

SUPPLIES:

Pencil and paper

Scissors

Hole punch

Hard felt, craft foam, or thin cardboard, in at least two colors

Craft glue

MISSION:

1. On a piece of paper, draw out the design you would like to use. Make sure it's at least half the length of the shoe you want to attach it to. This will be your stencil, so take your time making it exactly what you want. If you need help, refer to the example shapes shown above. (Flames add speed and power; wings, of course, add flight. Choose wisely.)

2. Before cutting out the stencil, hold it up to the shoes you will be decorating. Align the design with the side of the shoe, and mark the top three lace holes.

3. Use scissors to cut out the stencil, and use a hole punch on the lace hole markings to make room for the laces to weave through.

4. Use the stencil to trace the design onto the hard felt. Trace two pieces—one for the outside of each shoe. Be sure to mark the lace holes. Cut along the lines you drew and punch holes for the laces.

5. If you choose to use more than one color, either trace the same shape again, making these pieces slightly smaller, or create a new stencil. Cut these designs out and glue them to the pieces made in the first color. (Be sure to glue them on the outside so they will be seen when the wings or flames are attached to the shoes.)

6. Allow the glue to dry completely before powering up your super shoes.

7. When the glue is dry, unlace the shoes down to the top three holes and re-lace them, pulling the laces through the holes in the hard felt designs as well as the regular shoe holes. Secure the laces at the top, as usual, and off you go!

30 SPECIALTY GEAR

From utility belts to supershields, superheroes have access to incredible specialty gear just for them. Of course, villains also have their own specialty gear (see Villain Weapons on page 56), but then you didn't sign up for this because you thought it would be easy, did you? Here are some plans for equipment currently under development. For gear you can make yourself, review the next several pages.

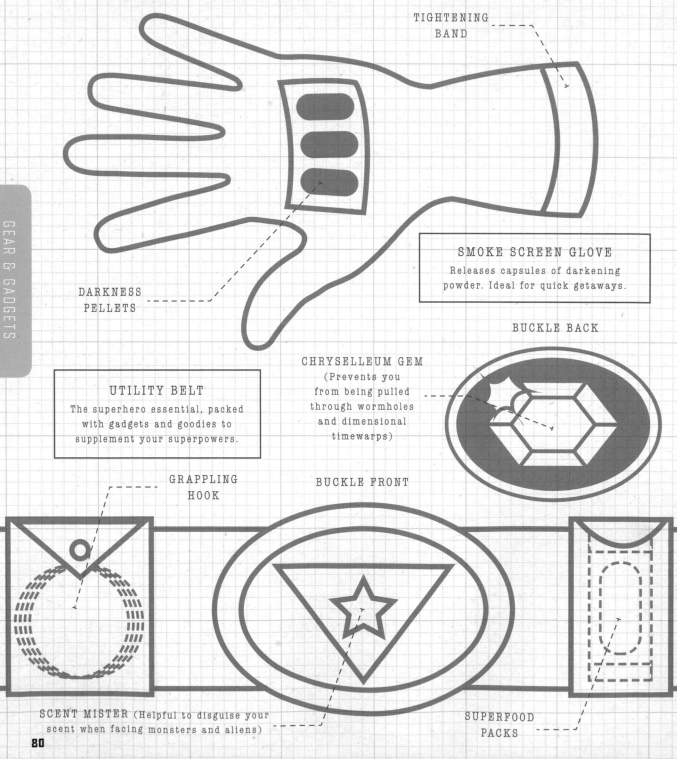

TIGHTENING BAND

DARKNESS PELLETS

SMOKE SCREEN GLOVE
Releases capsules of darkening powder. Ideal for quick getaways.

BUCKLE BACK

UTILITY BELT
The superhero essential, packed with gadgets and goodies to supplement your superpowers.

CHRYSELLEUM GEM (Prevents you from being pulled through wormholes and dimensional timewarps)

GRAPPLING HOOK

BUCKLE FRONT

SCENT MISTER (Helpful to disguise your scent when facing monsters and aliens)

SUPERFOOD PACKS

GEAR & GADGETS

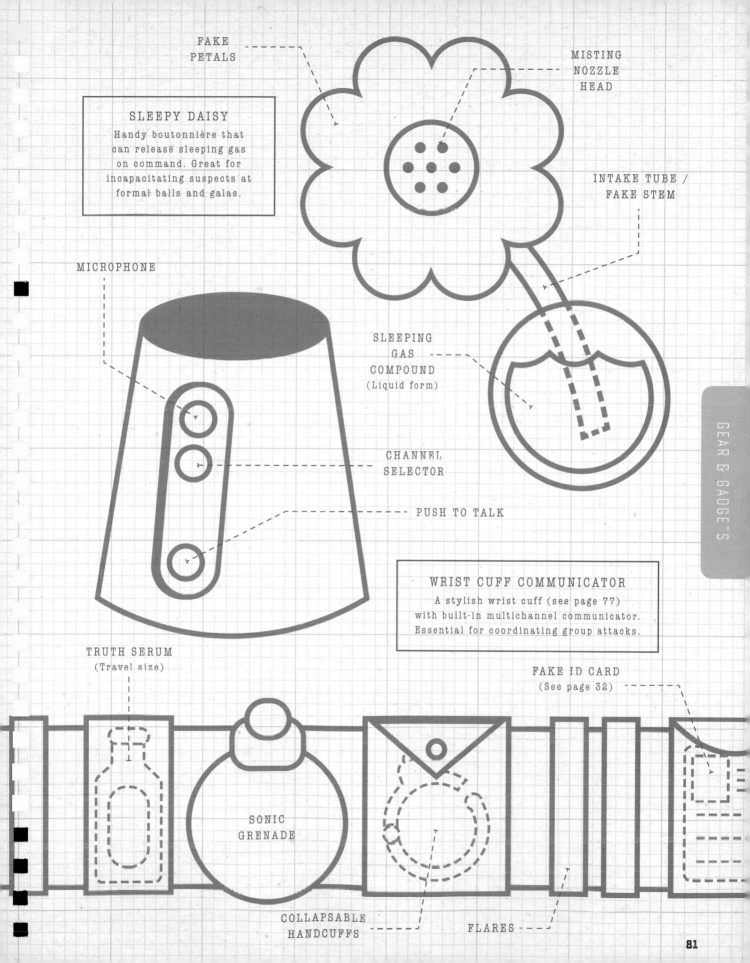

FAKE PETALS

MISTING NOZZLE HEAD

SLEEPY DAISY
Handy boutonnière that can release sleeping gas on command. Great for incapacitating suspects at formal balls and galas.

INTAKE TUBE / FAKE STEM

MICROPHONE

SLEEPING GAS COMPOUND (Liquid form)

CHANNEL SELECTOR

PUSH TO TALK

WRIST CUFF COMMUNICATOR
A stylish wrist cuff (see page 77) with built-in multichannel communicator. Essential for coordinating group attacks.

TRUTH SERUM (Travel size)

FAKE ID CARD (See page 32)

SONIC GRENADE

COLLAPSABLE HANDCUFFS

FLARES

30.2 MAKE YOUR OWN UTILITY BELT

SUPPLIES:

Old leather belt (buckle removed)

Permanent marker

Velcro strips

Felt or craft foam in bold colors

Assorted containers (cylindrical candy containers, mint tins, Silly String cans, etc.)

Craft glue

MISSION:

Wrap the belt around your waist (or the waist of the superhero) to measure the fit. Use a dark-colored permanent marker to mark the overlapping section on the inside of the belt.

Attach Velcro strips to the belt at the overlap to the keep the belt in place. Attach a second set of strips, if necessary, to hold the extra belt material in place. (If you have strong scissors, you can always trim off the excess length.) Be sure to attach the Velcro strips to the outside edge and one to the inside edge of the other end so the strips align.

Using felt, create a stylish belt buckle (preferably using your super logo and suit colors). Use one large shape as the base and then glue other shapes and designs on top. Make the buckle large enough to completely cover the belt.

Secure the logo to the belt with glue *or*, to make interchangeable buckles, add a Velcro strip to the back of the felt buckle and another corresponding strip to the leather belt. Create as many designs as you'd like, and simply add a Velcro strip to the back to attach.

To add compartments and gadgets to the belt, glue an assortment of containers at regular intervals around the belt. Allow the glue to dry at least 30 minutes before wearing the belt into action.

TIP: Be sure to keep your most-used items in easy-to-reach containers on your dominant side.

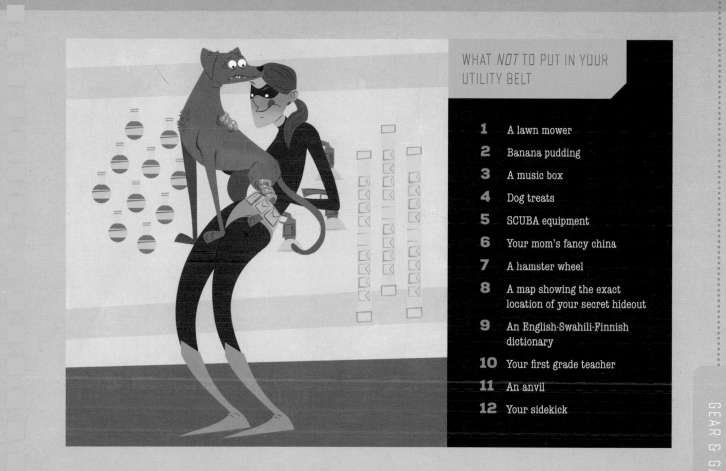

WHAT *NOT* TO PUT IN YOUR UTILITY BELT

1 A lawn mower

2 Banana pudding

3 A music box

4 Dog treats

5 SCUBA equipment

6 Your mom's fancy china

7 A hamster wheel

8 A map showing the exact location of your secret hideout

9 An English-Swahili-Finnish dictionary

10 Your first grade teacher

11 An anvil

12 Your sidekick

POWER BOOSTERS

COILED "ROPE"

The **Enquirer**

OFFICAL PHOTOGRAPHER'S PASS

NAME

ID NO. 4982

NINJA STARS

#GJE-S35

WHAT TO PUT IN YOUR UTILITY BELT

YOUR FAKE IDENTITY CARD (SEE PAGE 32)

MINI COMPASS

30.3 SUPER VISION PERISCOPE

Not every super is blessed with X-ray vision, so when you need a better view, pull out your trusty periscope.

SUPPLIES:

Large piece of cardboard

Ruler

Pen or pencil

X-Acto or craft knife

Two 3x3–inch mirrors
(available at craft stores)

Craft glue

Packing or duct tape

Empty toilet paper tube

Silver spray paint

Various decorations

MISSION:

1 Cut the cardboard into a rectangle that is 16 inches wide and 10.5 inches tall.

2 Place a ruler vertically along the left side of the cardboard and make a marking at 2.25 inches, 5.25 inches, and 7.5 inches. Make another set of markings halfway across the cardboard, and another set at the far right.

PEER OVER FENCES, TABLES, WALLS, AND OTHER BARRIERS WITH YOUR HANDY PERISCOPE. PEEK RESPONSIBLY!

TOP VIEW PORT (OPPOSITE SIDE)

CALIBRATION KNOBS

VIEW PORT

PERISCOPE HANDLES

3 Turn the ruler horizontally. Line it up with each set of markings and carefully connect the markings with a long horizontal line from the left of the cardboard to the right. Do this for each set of markings. This will create 4 rows on your cardboard: the first and third (A and C) will be 2.25 inches tall, and the second and fourth (B and D) will be 3 inches tall.

4 Using an X-Acto knife and a ruler, carefully score the cardboard along each line. Be sure to not let the knife cut all the way through the cardboard!

5 At the left side of row B and right side of row D, draw a rectangle that is 1.5 inches wide and 2.25 inches tall. Make sure each rectangle is about .5 inches from the edge of the cardboard. Carefully cut out each rectangle. You should now have something that looks similar to the image "Finished Cardboard."

6 Flip the cardboard over so the scored lines are on the bottom side. Glue one side of each of the mirrors according to Figure A.

7 Fold the cardboard up and glue the remaining sides of the mirrors. Secure the two ends of cardboard with packing or duct tape.

8 Cut the toilet paper tube in half. Glue each half of the tube on either side of the base of the periscope to serve as handles.

9 Paint the periscope silver. Allow to dry, then decorate with knobs, controls, and other embellishments.

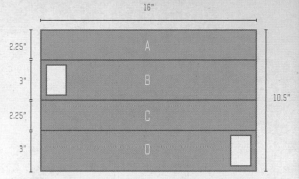

SCORING

FINISHED CARDBOARD

ADDING MIRRORS

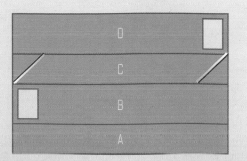

FIGURE A (CARDBOARD FLIPPED)

FOLDING AND TAPING

LITTLE-KNOWN USES FOR A SUPERSHIELD

A supershield is an invaluable asset in the battle against evil. But have you ever wondered what to do with your shield on your days off? In a pinch, your shield can double as any of the following:

BABY CRADLE

WOK PAN

SOUP DISH

SLED

30.4 MAKE YOUR OWN SUPERSHIELD

Most superheroes need a good supershield in the fight against villainy. Create your own and customize the colors and design to match your supersuit.

SUPPLIES:

Frisbee

Felt (enough to cover Frisbee, create handle, and add other designs)

Craft foam

Hot glue gun and glue sticks

MISSION:

1 Measure a circle of felt large enough to cover the entire front of the Frisbee and wrap around the edges. Lay the felt out on a flat surface, front side down.

2 Draw several lines on the front of Frisbee with hot glue and place immediately (face down) in the center of the felt circle. Press down for 5 to 10 seconds to secure.

3 When the front is secure, draw a line of hot glue along the inside edge of the Frisbee, and press the extra material down into the glue to attach.

TIP: Start on one edge, glue down a few inches, and then move to the opposite edge, stretching the material just slightly to ensure the fit is tight. Continue, working with 3-inch intervals at a time, until the entire edge is attached.

---

4 OPTIONAL: Cut a second circle to cover the inside face of the Frisbee and hot glue to attach.

5 Cut an 8-inch strip of craft foam (1–3 inches wide) to use as the handle. With the Frisbee still face down, place a pea-sized dot of glue on the top inch of the strip. Fold back the remaining fabric and attach the glued tab toward the top half of the Frisbee back. Press down for 5 seconds to secure.

6 Place another pea-sized dot of hot glue on the other end of the strip. Again, crease and fold the last inch underneath the rest of the handle. Press and hold to secure.

TIP: Two evenly-spaced handles will allow the wearer to hold the shield with his or her forearm instead of just with the hand.

---

7 While the glue dries, create your logo or other design in bright, bold colors. Turn the Frisbee right-side up and attach additional decoration with hot glue. (Don't use too much when attaching felt to felt. Small dots or thin lines will suffice.)

8 Allow the glue to set at least one hour before taking the shield into battle.

ATTACHING THE FELT

SECURING THE HANDLE

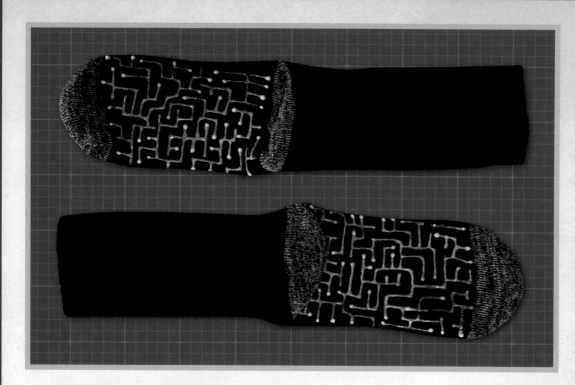

✂ 30.5 SUPER SPEED GRIP SOCKS

No superhero should be slipping and sliding around when there's evil afoot! Get a grip with these awesome super-grip socks.

SUPPLIES:

Mid-rise socks (pre-washed), any color

3-D paint (slick or puff paint), multiple colors

Stencils (optional)

MISSION:

1 Be sure to wash the socks before beginning. (This will help the paint to stick—and improve the smell . . .)

2 Using the 3-D paint, create super designs on the bottoms of both socks. Hold the paint bottle at a 45-degree angle and apply slowly. Use stencils or create your own designs freehand. Apply thick lines for maximum grip.

3 Allow the paint to dry at least 4 hours before donning the latest in anti-slip technology.

TIP: After use, wait 24 hours before washing and be sure to wash the socks inside out to avoid cracking.

PATTERN EXAMPLES:

A: SUPERHERO LOGO

B: RADIATION

C: FLAMES

ICE

STAINLESS STEEL

GLASS

MARBLE FLOORS

TOPS OF CARS

WET ROCKS

GEAR & GADGETS

SUPER PROFILE: DOUBLE TIME

Double Time (barely caught here on film) can run upwards of 700 mph. He set the world record for all track events in the 1984 Olympics as a 12-year-old. A few years later, he changed his name and began training to join up with the superheroes under the super name Double Time. At his fastest speeds, he is virtually invisible and has even been known to run across water. His quick speed is matched only by his quick wit. If you're going to banter with him, you'd better have a ready list of quick catchphrases at your disposal (see page 134).

GUIDELINES FOR USING TRUTH SERUM

1 Be persistent. Truth serum does work, but you'll often have to repeat your question multiple times before you get a complete answer. A series of Yes/No questions, rather than broad, open-ended questions, often works the best.

2 Be sure the villain is truly under the influence of the serum before questioning as villains have been known to fake their way through an interrogation with false answers. Common indicators of genuine truth serum response include unfocused eyes, unrelenting hiccups, change of hair color, and breath that smells like baby skunk.

3 Be prepared for what truths the villain reveals—it might be more than you bargained for. If you're thin-skinned or are having a bad hair day, you might want to turn the interrogation over to someone else.

SUPPLIES:

2 cups heavy cream

2 cups whole milk

3/4 cup sugar

2 teaspoons vanilla

Pinch of sea salt

Assorted food colorings

MISSION:

1 In a large bowl, whisk together all the ingredients (except food colorings) until the sugar is dissolved. Divide into three bowls and add a different food coloring to each. Pour into three 1-quart zip-close freezer bags and seal. Lay flat in the freezer for at least 2 hours.

2 Remove from freezer. Crumble and place each color of ice cream into a food processor, one color at a time, washing bowl thoroughly in between colors. Process until creamy and smooth. Drink through a straw like a milkshake or serve in bowl for soft-serve ice cream.

SERVES 2

Note how the use of open-ended questions got the superhero into hot water—a LOT of hot water.

Official Transcript of Interrogation

Villain: The Dark Demolisher
Interrogating Super: Gnatman
Date: October 26, 2002
Time: 23:34

G: The Dark Demolisher was captured today at 18:00 hours. Suspect still refuses to reveal the location of the bomb. Administering the truth serum now.

DD: I'll never tell you! The city will crumble and burn before I say a word!

G: Serum should take effect in 3 . . . 2 . . . 1 . . .

DD: My father never took me to the zoo when I was a child.

G: Tell us where you've hidden the bomb.

DD: I never liked the taste of cotton candy.

G: Is the bomb at city hall? At the opera house? Somewhere in the business district?

DD: I have to be honest, Gnatman; that color really isn't flattering for your complexion. I'd go with a dark maroon instead of that gaudy purple.

G: How long do we have until the bomb goes off?

DD: And I know we just spent the day battling, but would it kill you to take a shower? My nostrils are positively burning! Again, just being honest.

G: Millions of lives are at stake here, Demolisher! Where is the bomb?

DD: Oh, that. It's in the basement of the power plant. But you know, I've been meaning to talk to you about your car. Do you know how much pollution that gas-guzzler spits into the atmosphere? How can I take over the world if there isn't a world to take over? Honestly.

G: Let the record show that the interrogation was successful. Alert the bomb squad and the mayor.

DD: So I was reading your blog the other day . . .

G: How do you turn this thing off?!

End of recording

SECRET MESSAGES

When you send a message to your sidekick, you can't risk that the information might fall into the wrong hands. Use one of these super-secret methods to make your messages indecipherable! (But be sure to let your sidekick know how to crack the code.)

3E.1 CREATE YOUR OWN SECRET MESSAGES

For a quick secret code, simply substitute a different letter, number, or shape (or a mixture of the three) for each letter of the alphabet.

For example, using the key to the right, the message "Send help now" would look like this:

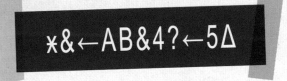

For practice, try decoding these other messages:

⊙ 5 C ⊙ 3 ✶ 3 ← 1 5 7 6 ! B 5 7 ✶ &

C & & ! C & → ! ✶ 7 ⊙ C → 6 3 ← &

? 6 & ✶ 3 A & ← ! 3 ← A → ← « & 6

? 6 5 ! & 1 ! ⊙ → ← < E → 7 4 !

→ ! ! → 1 < → ! C 3 A ← 3 « B !

→ 6 & ¢ 5 7 & E & ← 6 & → A 3 ← « ! B 3 ✶

CONFIDENTIAL
TOP SECRET

SUPPLIES:

2 cups ABC-shaped cereal

2 cups yogurt-covered mini pretzels

1 cup dried cranberries

1 cup pretzel M&M's

1 cup gummy ABCs

MISSION:

1 Combine all ingredients in a large zip-close plastic bag and seal securely. SHAKE!

2 Divide evenly among your superhero friends to figure out the "secret message."

SERVES 4-6

#GK-1   UNSCRAMBLE THE SECRET MESSAGES

KATCAT _____

ORMEOVE _____

EEOITHAGNMTON _____

_____

ANSWERS: ATTACK, COVER ME, MEETING AT NOON

∃E.∃ MYSTERY MESSAGE CAKE

SUPPLIES:

3 packages yellow or golden yellow cake mixes (butter recipe)

3 packages (8 ounces each) cream cheese, room temperature

1 1/2 cups granulated sugar

1 1/2 cups water

12 large eggs

3 tablespoons vanilla

1 small jar of red paste food coloring

1 jar purchased vanilla frosting

Assorted sprinkles (optional)

Fondant (optional)

MISSION:

1 Preheat oven to 350 degrees. Line three 8x8-inch square pans with parchment paper leaving 2 inches on each end to hang over the sides. Set aside until ready to use.

2 Mix 1 package of cake mix, adding 1 package cream cheese, 1/2 cup sugar, 1/2 cup water, 4 eggs, and the entire jar of food coloring into a mixing bowl. Beat with an electric mixer for 3 to 5 minutes or until smooth and creamy. Divide batter evenly between two pans, filling 3/4 full.

3 Bake for 30 minutes or until light golden brown. Remove from oven and cool in pans for 15 minutes before removing to wire racks and cooling completely. Once the cakes have completely cooled, trim off the top slightly to form a flat surface. Cut out three letters to make your message with 2-inch cookie cutters and set aside until ready to use.

4 Mix the remaining two packages of cake mix according to package directions, adding 2 packages of cream cheese, 1 cup of sugar, 1 cup of water, 8 eggs, and 2 tablespoons vanilla. Pour about 1 inch of the batter into the third prepared pan. Insert the first row of letters to spell your secret message. Space the remaining letters behind each other as close as possible without any gaps.

5 Fill a piping bag with remaining batter and pipe the batter around each letter, filling 3/4 full. Smooth over batter with a spatula, making sure all letters are completely covered.

6 Bake for 30 minutes or until light golden brown. Remove from oven and cool in pan for 15 minutes before removing to wire rack and cooling completely.

7 Once completely cooled, trim the cake sides and top using a serrated knife to ensure a perfectly sized cake with the lettering centered.

8 Frost and decorate with sprinkles or fondant.

SERVES 12

WORKOUT ROUTINE
Keep your moves quick and strong with regular conditioning.

BODYWEIGHT SQUATS

MOUNTAIN CLIMBERS

LEG RAISES

CHAIR DIPS

TOE CRUNCHES

HIGH KNEES

CHAPTER FOUR

4

MOVES
&
MANEUVERS

FLYING

Bird or plane, flying is an essential skill for many superheroes. Though not strictly necessary to be successful, learning to master the techniques of flying can make a huge difference in battle.

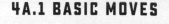

4A.1 BASIC MOVES

THE ARROW

Stretch out your arms in classic superhero style. Great for photoshoots and airplane fly-bys (just stay away from those engines!).

THE ROCKET

Flatten your arms to your sides and make yourself as streamlined as possible for maximum speed.

THE BACKSTROKE

Rotate your arms just like the traditional swimming stroke. Especially helpful if you need to keep an eye on your pursuers—or want an easy way to taunt them.

FREESTYLE

Also commonly called falling (which, in case you didn't know, is never a good situation to be in). If you find do yourself in such a predicament, remember that flapping your arms never helps. Ever.

Note: Flying is best attempted without capes attached (unless, of course, you're doing a photoshoot or filming a commercial).

4A.2 THINGS TO AVOID IN THE AIR

You might feel free in that wide open space, but don't believe for a second that the air is free of danger. When you fly, be sure to keep a close lookout for any of these common encounters.

PIGEONS

AIRPLANE ENGINES

THUNDERHEADS

MAGIC CARPETS

BIRTHDAY BALLOONS

FLOATING ISLANDS

FIREWORKS

MONUMENTS

SMOKESTACKS

PTERODACTYLS

TELEPHONE WIRES

SUPER PROFILE: NIMBUS

Many superheroes can fly, but there's no one faster than Nimbus. His ability to warp energy fields enables him to fly at speeds exceeding the speed of light itself. Most experts agree that he can fly fast enough to travel back through time, but no one has yet tested the theory (and Nimbus isn't interested in wearing 18th-century clothes anyway).

TRANSPORTATION

The world of transportation for superheroes is a beautiful, adrenaline-pumping place. As you consider forms of transportation, be sure to select something that complements your style, your powers, and your general location.

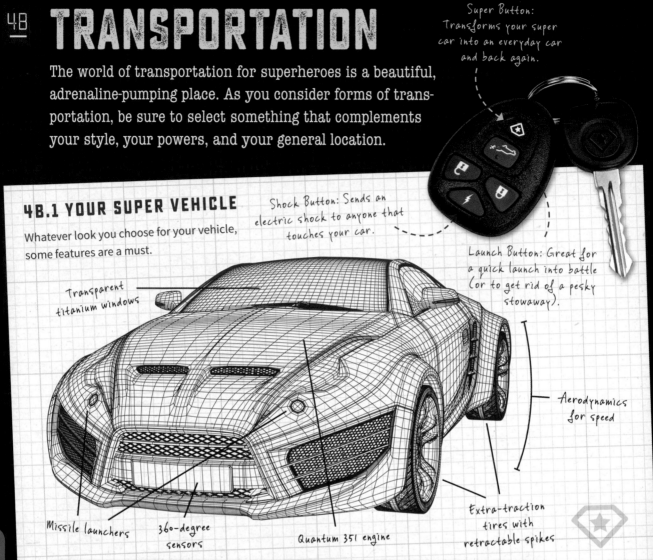

Super Button: Transforms your super car into an everyday car and back again.

48.1 YOUR SUPER VEHICLE

Whatever look you choose for your vehicle, some features are a must.

Shock Button: Sends an electric shock to anyone that touches your car.

Launch Button: Great for a quick launch into battle (or to get rid of a pesky stowaway).

Transparent titanium windows

Aerodynamics for speed

Missile launchers

360-degree sensors

Quantum 351 engine

Extra-traction tires with retractable spikes

Hopefully this list is obvious to you, but in case it's not, we'll save you some major embarrassment (and help you arrive on time).

WHAT *NOT* TO USE FOR TRANSPORTATION

1 Horse and buggy

2 Hot air balloon

3 Tricycle

4 Rickshaw

5 Giant slingshot

6 Cable car

7 Ice cream truck (though your fellow supers might forgive you on this one)

4B.2 MAPPING THE QUICKEST ROUTE

When you're after a villain and time is of the essence, smart navigation can mean everything. Review the GPS map below and chart the fastest path to the villain. Watch out for obstacles that might cause major delays!

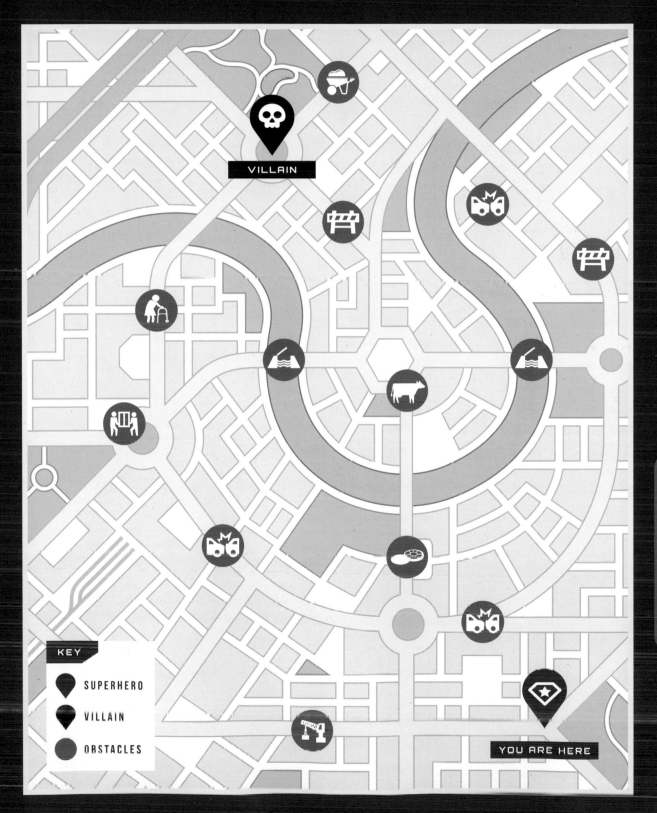

MARKSMANSHIP

Time and ammo are precious, so hit your target right the first time. As with all super-hero skills, good marksmanship is a matter of practice, practice, practice!

MOVES & MANEUVERS

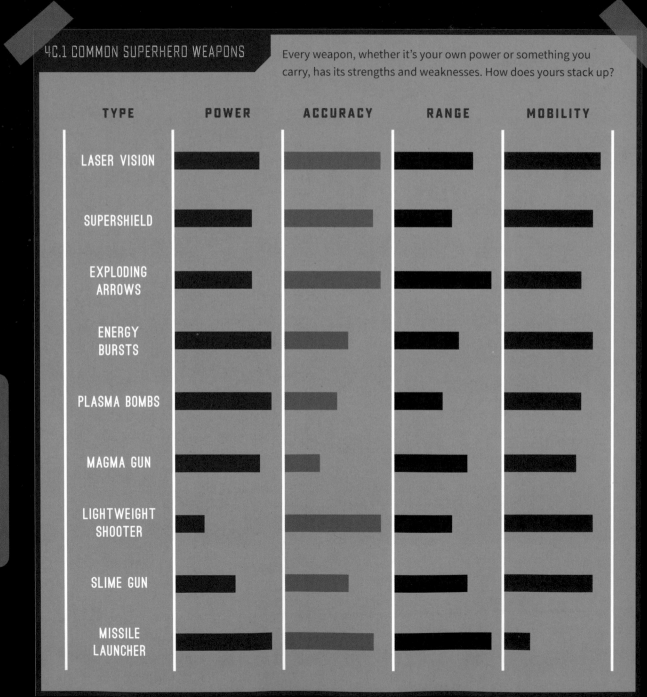

4C.1 COMMON SUPERHERO WEAPONS

Every weapon, whether it's your own power or something you carry, has its strengths and weaknesses. How does yours stack up?

TYPE	POWER	ACCURACY	RANGE	MOBILITY
LASER VISION				
SUPERSHIELD				
EXPLODING ARROWS				
ENERGY BURSTS				
PLASMA BOMBS				
MAGMA GUN				
LIGHTWEIGHT SHOOTER				
SLIME GUN				
MISSILE LAUNCHER				

TARGET PRACTICE

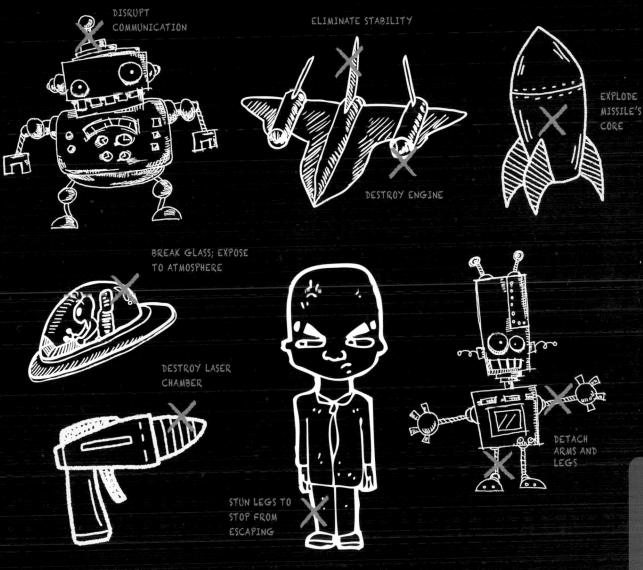

DISRUPT COMMUNICATION

ELIMINATE STABILITY

DESTROY ENGINE

EXPLODE MISSILE'S CORE

BREAK GLASS; EXPOSE TO ATMOSPHERE

DESTROY LASER CHAMBER

DETACH ARMS AND LEGS

STUN LEGS TO STOP FROM ESCAPING

SUPER PROFILE: SIGHTS

Born to a physicist mother and a major general father, Sights has the best markmanship among today's superheroes. At age 5, she could nail flies from across the room with rubber bands. By age 9, she had started rifle shooting and was already winning national competitions. She signed up to fight evil at age 13, completed her training by age 16, and became one of the youngest—and most accurate—superheroes ever by age 17. It's best to make sure you're on her good side—all the time.

4C.2 BULL'S-EYE YOGURT DIP

SUPPLIES:

1 quart plain Greek yogurt

2 tablespoons maple syrup or honey

1 tablespoon vanilla

1/4 teaspoon ground cinnamon

Red and blue food coloring

MISSION:

1 In the yogurt container, mix the yogurt with maple syrup or honey, vanilla, and cinnamon. Divide evenly between three bowls, leaving one plain and coloring one blue and the other red.

2 Use two round sugar cookie cutters to create the bull's-eye, one smaller than the other. Place the smaller cutter in the center of a bowl and spoon in the red yogurt. Place the larger cookie-cutter around the smaller in the bowl. Spoon in the plain white yogurt. Lastly, fill the outer ring with the blue yogurt.

3 Place the bowl in the freezer for about 30 minutes to firm up yogurt. Remove from freezer and carefully remove the cookie cutters.

SERVES 4

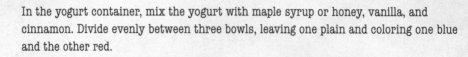

4C.3 CINNAMON ARROW CHIPS

SUPPLIES:

3 (6–8 inch) whole wheat pitas

1–2 tablespoons olive oil

1/2 cup sugar

1 teaspoon ground cinnamon

MISSION:

1 Preheat oven to 375 degrees. Line a baking sheet with foil and set aside until ready to use.

2 Cut each pita into arrow shapes with a small cookie cutter. Brush lightly with olive oil, mix sugar and cinnamon in a bowl, and sprinkle the mixture evenly over the pita pieces.

3 Arrange on prepared baking sheet and bake about 6 to 10 minutes or until golden brown. Remove from oven and cool a few minutes before eating.

Best used the day made.

SERVES 4

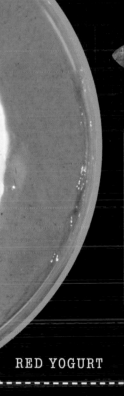

INCOMING CINNAMON ARROW CHIPS

RED YOGURT

PLAIN YOGURT

BLUE YOGURT

40 | SMASHING

Every superhero faces a challenge just on the other side of a wall or obstacle. And sometimes, to alleviate the stresses of superhero life, you just need to smash something (without hurting anyone, of course).

BRICK

For the best results, get a running (or flying) start toward the wall before smashing through. Fist first, rather than head first, is preferred.

GLASS

If you have a sonic soundwave emitter in your utility belt (or a very nice singing voice), high-pitched frequencies will effectively shatter glass.

WOOD

A solid punch should do the trick, but watch out for splinters.

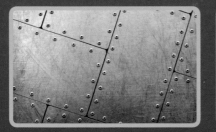

TITANIUM STEEL

This will take a bit of extra effort, but with the right force and while wearing the right footwear, a strong superhero can smash through even titanium-plated armor.

MOVIE THEATER SCREEN

If you like to make an entrance, be sure to wait until a point in the movie that will convince the audience that their 3-D glasses are working a little too well.

ICE

If possible, wear protective goggles if you plan to smash your way through. Ice tends to shatter, and flying shards are just as deadly as knives. A quick blast with your laser vision will melt it much more safely.

SAND

Sorry, you can't punch your way through sand. However, a shovel (and a willing sidekick) will really come in handy.

CONCRETE

Smashing concrete tends to stir up clouds of dust. If you wear a dark-colored supersuit, be sure to dust yourself off before signing autographs for your adoring fans.

PLASTIC

Most supers underestimate the strength of plastic. Whether you choose to puncture or smash the material, be sure to recycle.

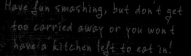

SMASH THAT GUACAMOLE!

Have fun smashing, but don't get too carried away or you won't have a kitchen left to eat in!

🍴 40.2 SMASH! GUACAMOLE

SUPPLIES:

1 avocado, peeled and pitted

1/4 cup whipped cream cheese

1 tablespoon lemon juice

1 tablespoon honey

Sea salt and pepper to taste

MISSION:

1 Place all of the ingredients in a bowl or zip-close plastic bag and mash together.

2 If using a plastic bag, snip off the corner and pipe into a bowl.

3 Serve with cut up veggies, fruits, crackers, or pretzels.

MAKES 1 CUP (ABOUT 2 SERVINGS)

MOVES & MANEUVERS

A favorite booster food among superheroes, and one created by their very own Aldente (see page 18).

Power up your punches big time with this delicious burrito bowl.

SUPPLIES:

3 cups brown rice, cooked

Juice of 1 lime

1 tablespoon olive oil

1/3 cup fresh cilantro, chopped

Corn chips (optional)

1 can (15 ounces) black beans, drained and rinsed

2 cups cooked, shredded chicken

2 avocados, sliced

3/4 cup salsa

1/2 cup plain Greek yogurt

Other optional toppings: fresh corn, chopped tomatoes, cheddar cheese

MISSION:

1. Place rice in a large bowl. Add lime juice, olive oil, and fresh cilantro. Toss to blend.

2. If using corn chips, place on bottom of six bowls. Divide the rice between the bowls, and top with black beans. Add shredded chicken and a layer of sliced avocado. Top with salsa and Greek yogurt. Add additional toppings of your choice.

MAKES 6 BOWLS

#GJE-S35

PUT THE POWER IN YOUR BOWL

A BROWN RICE: A GREAT SOURCE OF ENERGY, PLUS EXTRA NUTRIENTS NOT FOUND IN WHITE RICE.

B BLACK BEANS: FULL OF PROTEIN, FIBER, AND NUTRIENTS.

C AVOCADO: PACKED WITH NEARLY 20 DIFFERENT VITAMINS, MINERALS, AND NUTRIENTS.

D GREEK YOGURT: FULL OF PROTEIN AND PROBIOTICS.

POWER BOWL

MOVES & MANEUVERS

40.4 HIGH-RISE BUILDING BLOCKS

When you aren't leaping over tall buildings in a single bound, use these high-rise models to plan your strategy for defending the city (or knocking it down).

SUPPLIES:

2"x4"s in various sizes*
Spray paint

Assorted colors of masking, painter's, electrical, or duct tape

MISSION:

1 Cut 2"x4"s into various lengths to create your superhero buildings. It may be necessary to sand the edges to provide a smooth, safe surface for superheroes' hands.

2 Spray paint buildings and allow paint to dry.

3 Decorate with assorted colors and sizes of tape to create windows, doors, and designs.

4 Stack 'em high and smash 'em down!

 *You can also look for pre-cut, pre-sanded blocks at your local craft store. Many stores carry an assortment of rectangles, cubes, and other fun shapes that are perfect for turning into city buildings.

BRICK HIGHLIGHTS

GRID WINDOWS

A-FRAME WINDOWS

SILLED WINDOWS

IDEAL TAPE COLORS

RED PAINTER'S TAPE: BRICK HIGHLIGHTS

BLUE PAINTER'S TAPE: WINDOWS

ELECTRICAL TAPE: ARCHITECTURAL DETAILS

MASKING TAPE: MASONRY

DESIGN IDEAS

4E FIGHTING

In addition to using traditional martial arts, superheroes have a few moves that are all their own. Consider this page taken from Madame Woo's now famous textbook:

═══ MADAME WOO'S SUPERHERO FIGHTING SCHOOL ═══

Figure 37. You must be strong as a cyclone, swift as a river, and decisive as a serpent. There is no place for flair, but power; is not the purple peacock devoured by the gray wolf?

Jumping Deer.

Translation: Hit the villain as hard as you can and hope they don't get back up. If they do, try again or select a different method of attack. Or run.

Flying Talon.

Translation: Jump and deliver a strong flying kick. Just try not to look like a ballet dancer in the process (unless, of course, you are one).

Falling Stone.

Translation: Drop down and hit the ground from above with the force of a freight train—one loaded with dynamite if you can manage it.

Tornado.

Translation: Spin around as quickly as possible with your fists extended. Should effectively incapacitate enemies within a 100-foot radius.

Hurling Ox.

Translation: Pick up something super heavy and hurl it at your enemies. Remember, bend with your knees!

Reverse Tornado.

Translation: Spin like the Tornado, only use your legs for attack instead of your fists.

Sly Opposum.

Translation: Say, "Look over there!" and punch the villain as hard as you can. Note: Usually only works once.

Candle of Anger.

Translation: Burst into flames and charge your enemies. Great for effect, but only works if you have this power.

TASTY, REFRESHING, AND THOROUGHLY PATRIOTIC

🍴 4E.2 1-2 "PUNCH" The perfect thirst-quencher after a long day of training.

SUPPLIES:

Ice cubes

1 bottle cranberry juice

1 bottle blue Gatorade

1 bottle strawberry sparkling water

MISSION:

1 Fill a glass with ice cubes.

2 Pour in the cranberry juice. Carefully add Gatorade, making sure to pour it directly onto the ice cubes or the juice will mix. Again, DO NOT MIX.

3 Pour in the sparkling water, making sure to pour directly over the ice cubes. Repeat to fill any additional glasses.

SERVES 12

4E.3 PUNCHING BAG PILLOW

As every good superhero knows, practice makes perfect. The key to the perfect punch is repetition, and since you won't always have a villain's evil henchmen handy, it's best to have your own practice equipment.

SUPPLIES:

Old throw pillow, any shape

Felt in two contrasting colors (preferably red and white, but any bold colors will do)

Scissors

Pins (optional)

Fabric glue (or hot glue gun)

MISSION:

1 Trace concentric circles in the bold-colored felts. Be sure the colors alternate, and make each circle smaller than the one before it. We recommend using about five circles—three from the red and two from the white—but you can make as many as you like.

TIP: Use nesting mixing bowls to trace perfect circles in different sizes. Use the largest bowl for the outside red ring, the next largest bowl for the outside white ring, and so on.

2 Cut out the circles and arrange them in a bull's-eye design on the pillow. Pin them in place if it makes it easier.

3 Draw a squiggly line of glue on the back of each circle and attach to the pillow one at a time, starting with the largest circle first and working to the smallest one last.

OPTIONAL: Cut a strip of felt, form into a loop, and glue both ends to the back of the pillow to allow the punching bag to be hung from a hook.

4 Allow the punching bag to dry completely (at least 3 hours) before commencing combat practice.

TRACE THE FIRST CIRCLE

GLUE FIRST CIRCLE SECURELY

REPEAT FOR REMAINING CIRCLES

4F JUMPING

Whether jumping to attack, evade, leap a building, or—let's face it—just look cool, proper technique makes all the difference.

HOW TO LEAP A BUILDING IN A SINGLE BOUND

1 Stand with your feet shoulder-width apart.

2 Bend your knees and squat low to the ground.

3 Jump!

4 Clear the building, keeping an eye out for cell phone towers and stray pigeons.

5 Land softly by bending your knees upon impact.

4F.1 FRUIT TOWERS

SUPPLIES:

3/4 cup peanut, almond, or sunflower butter, or Nutella

2 apples, cored and cut into ten rings, each about 1/4 inch thick

4 tablespoons granola

2 tablespoons dried fruits

MISSION:

1 Spread 4 tablespoons of peanut butter onto half of the apple rings. Sprinkle each with 1 tablespoon of granola and some dried fruits (e.g., raisins, dates, etc.). Cover each with one of the remaining apple rings to form sandwiches.

2 Repeat and stack as many and as high as desired.

SERVES 2

JUMPING TIPS

1 Look before you leap. Literally.

2 Land on soft surfaces as often as possible, with the exception of garbage heaps, tigers, and quicksand. Though soft landings, those never turn out well.

3 Make sure your belongings are properly secured before jumping. Nothing ruins a super's day more than dropping his or her favorite blaster from 50 stories up.

MOVES & MANEUVERS

Jumping across flames, lava, toxic waste, and other dangerous substances requires focus and great accuracy. If the area is too large to jump across in one leap, you'll need to use anchors (such as rocks, debris, and other sturdy materials) to navigate across. Note: Jumping onto a sinking object seconds before it disappears may look cool on film, but in real life, it usually doesn't turn out well.

(HOSTAGE IN DISTRESS)

MOVES & MANEUVERS

4F.2 MOLTEN S'MORES

SUPPLIES:

1 cup milk chocolate chips

1 cup mini marshmallows

Galactic Graham Crackers (see 4F.3)

MISSION:

1 Preheat oven to 450 degrees. Place chocolate evenly on the bottom of an 8- to 10-inch cast iron skillet or oven-safe baking dish of the approximate size.

2 Sprinkle marshmallows on top of chocolate chips.

3 Bake for 7 to 9 minutes or until the marshmallows turn golden brown.

4 Serve with Galactic Graham Crackers as dippers.

SERVES 2

4F.3 GALACTIC GRAHAM CRACKERS

SUPPLIES:

1 cup whole wheat flour

1 1/2 cups all purpose flour

1/2 cup dark brown sugar, packed

1/2 teaspoon salt

1 teaspoon cinnamon

1 teaspoon baking soda

1/2 cup butter, chilled and cubed

1/4 cup honey

1/4 cup water

MISSION:

1 Preheat oven to 350 degrees. Line a sheet pan with parchment paper or foil and set aside until ready to use.

2 Combine the first six ingredients in a large bowl. Add cubed and chilled butter and mix with your fingers until it is combined.

3 Stir in honey and water and mix with a spoon until it begins to form a dough ball.

4 Flatten dough into a disc and roll out 1/4-inch thick on floured work area. Cut out crackers with cookie cutters and place on prepared sheet pan. Bake for 15 minutes, remove from oven, and cool 5 minutes before removing from sheet pan. Store in an airtight container when cooled.

Tip: To create the characters on the left, cut out the graham crackers using people-shaped cookie cutters. Decorate the cooled cookies with colored fondant and icing.

SERVES 2

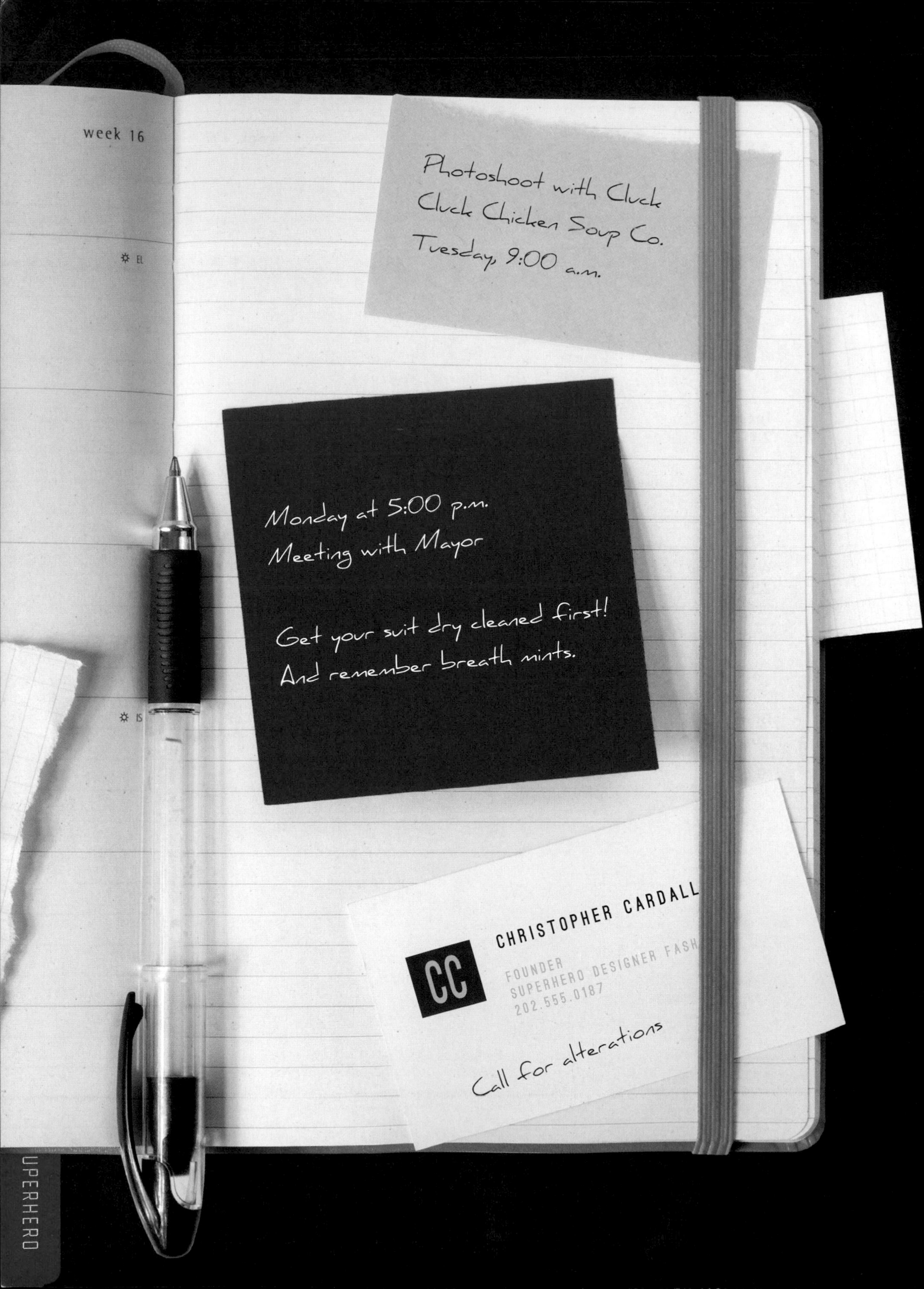

Photoshoot with Cluck
Cluck Chicken Soup Co.
Tuesday, 9:00 a.m.

Monday at 5:00 p.m.
Meeting with Mayor

Get your suit dry cleaned first!
And remember breath mints.

CHRISTOPHER CARDALL

CC FOUNDER
SUPERHERO DESIGNER FASH
202.555.0187

Call for alterations

5

BEING A SUPERHERO

5A FINDING YOUR SUPERPOWERS

5A.1 THE JOURNEY OF A THOUSAND MILES BEGINS WITH ONE STEP

Superheroes are, well, super, and that's usually by virtue of how they've discovered and harnessed their superpowers. Discovering your own superpowers can take time. For some, it happens purely by accident. For others, it's a matter of fate and destiny. In either case, with great power comes great responsibility. Use the tools on these pages to find your own powers, then move through the chapter to develop them and begin your training.

5A.2 HOW TO DISCOVER YOUR OWN SUPERPOWER

If you know you're destined for greatness but haven't seen evidence of superpowers yet, you're not alone. Some superheroes can feel their super-potential long before their actual powers kick in, but that's not to say there's nothing you can do about it.

To determine your own superpower, take a moment to think back on recent experiences. If you recently blasted a hole in the wall when you sneezed, you may have super strength. If you recently convinced a dog to eat your homework, you might be able to communicate with animals. If you recently saw the cookies your mom hid through the cupboard door, you may have X-ray vision. Take note of your unique abilities—they just might be the first signs of your superpower.

But above all, don't force it. Most superheroes discover their powers completely by accident. Your superpowers will make themselves known when the time is right.

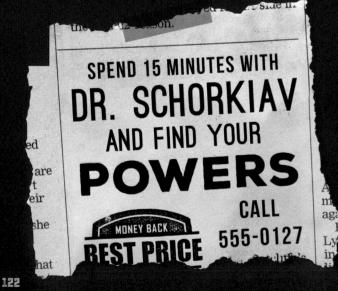

SPEND 15 MINUTES WITH
DR. SCHORKIAV
AND FIND YOUR
POWERS
CALL
555-0127
MONEY BACK
BEST PRICE

SUPERPOWER FRAUD

Resist services that promise to help you discover your superpowers. Even at the best of times, these are run by wacky, renegade doctors. And at the worst of times? These are produced by villains looking to ensnare future henchmen. It's tempting to want to know your powers now, but be patient and let things take the proper course. You can't force greatness.

POWER	DESCRIPTION	USUAL METHOD OF DISCOVERY	PROS	CONS
Flight	The ability to defy gravity and propel oneself through the air	Daydreaming you can fly, when suddenly . . .	• Quick and easy form of transportation • Never wait in another airport security line	• Swallowing bugs • Thunderstorms
Super Speed	The ability to run at speeds physically impossible for the typical human body	Rushing when late for second period	• Perfectly punctual • Chores take a fraction of the time (i.e., more time for fun)	• No way to avoid messy/wind-blown hair • Eventual loss of patience with the agonizingly slow pace of the rest of the world
Super Strength	The ability to apply and exert force far greater than the typical human capacity	Attempting to lift a really heavy backpack	• Always win at tug-of-war or arm wrestling • Easily create doors and windows by smashing through, well, anything	• Extremely difficult to handle fragile objects like kittens or your mom's china • Everyone wants you to help them move their furniture
Animal Characteristics	The ability to adopt various characteristics of a specific animal, typically felines, insects, or reptiles	A trip to a zoo or an animal testing lab	• Heightened senses, balance, and speed • Easy to choose your superhero name (e.g., Tiger Woman, Birdboy, etc.)	• Hairballs, dry skin, and other inconveniences that come with animal behavior • Possible urge to become a vegetarian
Invisibility	The ability to hide oneself from the naked eye	Feeling a strong sense of embarrassment (i.e., wishing to disappear)	• Anonymity • Perfect hiding place—anyplace	• Must be wearing a special suit (. . . or your "birthday suit") • Easily ignored or forgotten (because no one saw you)
Telepathy/ Telekinesis	The ability to communicate (telepath) and/or manipulate/move objects (telekinetic) with one's mind	Telepathy: Trying to get a friend's attention Telekinesis: Watching *Star Wars*	• Very subtle • No need to get your hands dirty	• Accidentally yelling in someone's head • Hitting yourself in the face with an object you summon too quickly

Over the years, some superheroes have emerged with powers that are out of the ordinary.

NEVER-BEFORE-SEEN POWERS!

THE WORLD'S GREATEST HEROES SHARE THEIR SECRETS

WE DON'T KNOW IF THEY'RE USEFUL, BUT THEY'RE **AWESOME!**

IN AN EXCLUSIVE INTERVIEW, 5 SECRET SUPERHEROES REVEAL THEIR HIDDEN POWERS FOR FIGHTING CRIME.

GRAMPS: A MEDICATION MIX-UP GAVE HIM THE STRENGTH AND VIGOR OF A SUPER 20-YEAR-OLD, BUT THE APPEARANCE OF A NON-SUPER 80-YEAR-OLD. ALWAYS UNDER-ESTIMATED BY HIS OPPONENTS AND ALWAYS VICTORIOUS. ATTRIBUTES HIS SUCCESS TO HIS PRUNE JIUCE REGIMEN.

RIGHT WHERE I LEFT YOU.

HOLE IN ONE: HAD AN ACCIDENT WHILE WORKING IN A GOLF CLUB FACTORY. ARMS AND LEGS NOW HAVE STEEL CORES AND SUPER STRENGTH (AND SUPERB BALANCE). FOR SOME STRANGE REASON, CAN NOW ALSO HIT A HOLE-IN-ONE FROM NEARLY ANY DISTANCE. FINALLY JOINED CRIME FIGHTING AFTER BEING BANNED FROM ALL PRO-GOLFING ORGANIZATIONS. SIDEKICK GOES BY "CADDY."

COMET TAIL: TRAVELED TO EARTH RIDING THE DUST TRAIL OF A COMET. USES PARTICLES OF DUST TO FLY, LEVITATE OBJECTS, AND MOVE THROUGH SPACE. WEAKNESS: FEATHER DUSTERS.

FUSION MAN: FIRST WORKED AS AN ASTRONAUT. WAS BURNED BY THE SUN'S RADIATION AND ACQUIRED ABILITY TO SHOOT FIREBALLS FROM HIS EARS AND NOSTRILS. STRANGE, BUT EFFECTIVE.

THE HIBERNATOR: CAN SLEEP THROUGH ANYTHING . . . LITERALLY. SUPERS QUESTION HIS ADMISSION TO THE FORCE, BUT HAVEN'T BEEN ABLE TO WAKEN HIM LONG ENOUGH TO VOICE THEIR OBJECTIONS.

Take a look at the powers chronicled on these pages and familiarize yourself with some of the incredible—and sometimes not-so-incredible—possibilities.

RAINBOY JOINS UP

April 7—Anonymous superhero sources have confirmed that Rainboy has joined the ranks of crime-fighting heroes. First discovered at age 5 living in the basement of an abandoned weather station, Rainboy has the unique ability to call down rain from skies above, be it sunny or cloudy. Some question what role this specific power could play in the fight against evil, but Rainboy's demolition of the head-

GREEN THUMB

More known for his, um, unconventional dress than his powers, Green Thumb can grow trees, flowers, and vegetables in almost any conditions. On the more helpful side, he is also a great shot with bow and arrow.

HANDSTAND

At just 4 feet tall and 6 years of age, Handstand is the youngest superhero on record. He can walk on his hands as easily as his feet, with a personal record of 35 hand-miles logged in one day. This was thought useless until the villain Footloose disabled the use of feet world-wide. Only Handstand was left standing to save the day, which he did.

BACONATOR

Baconator can turn anything he touches into bacon. Conventional superheroes approved his admission to the ranks mostly because it made breakfast easy, but Baconator's skills have been surprisingly useful in fights against villains. It turns out that even they can't resist the lure of crisp, delicious bacon. Who can?

MISS CANINE

Miss Canine can transform into a dog (and back, thank goodness). This has proven useful for spying, but is rather limiting when it comes to battling robots and invading aliens. Both appear to be immune to fleas.

Other Unusual Powers on Record:

- **Parabola:** Can compute complex equations in her head.
- **Time Table:** Always knows the exact time of anywhere in the world, even with daylight savings time.
- **The Hare:** Runs at speeds close to Double Time (see page 89), but also has an endearing tail and whiskers.
- **Granite Man:** Can turn into a block of gray granite, but can't move afterwards until changing back.
- **Veganator:** Twin sister to Baconator. Can turn anything she touches into leafy green vegetables. The sibling rivalry is intense, but put to good use by the superhero community.

5A.5 HOW TO DEVELOP YOUR SUPERPOWERS

Once you have discovered your superpower, it is up to you to practice and develop that power.

EXAMPLES OF HOW TO DEVELOP YOUR POWERS

FOR SUPER STRENGTH: Set a goal to lift increasingly heavy objects, starting with milk cartons and moving up to dressers and parked cars. (Remember, lift with your knees, not your back.)

SERVES 2

5A.6 POWER-BOOSTING SMOOTHIES

Boost your superpowers with these delicious smoothies. Choose from one of the recipes below, depending on what power-up you're looking for.

SUPPLIES:

BERRY BOOSTER SMOOTHIE

1 cup blueberries
1/2 cup strawberries
1/2 cup raspberries

1 cup milk of choice
1 tablespoon nut or seed butter
1/2 teaspoon almond extract

LIME-GREEN ENERGY SMOOTHIE

1 cup milk of choice
1 cup baby spinach
1/2 cup frozen strawberries
1/2 cup frozen peaches

1/2 avocado or banana
Juice of 1/2 fresh lime
Dash of nutmeg or cinnamon
Honey or maple syrup to taste

IMMUNITY ORANGE SMOOTHIE

1/2 cup plain Greek yogurt
1/2 banana, sliced and frozen
1/2 cup fresh orange juice

1/2 cup frozen mango or pineapple cubes
1/2 teaspoon vanilla
Honey or maple syrup to taste

POWER-UP POTENTIAL KEY

INCREASES IMMUNITY

BOOSTS SUPER STRENGTH

BOOSTS LASER & X-RAY VISION

ENHANCES ALL SUPERPOWERS

MISSION:

1   Blend and serve.

FOR TELEKINESIS: Place a small object on the other side of the room and focus all your thoughts and energy on summoning it to you. Don't blink. (This might take a while.)

FOR SUPER SPEED: Mark out a race course in your yard or a nearby park, and time yourself running the same stretch every day for a week. Take note of your progress. (Consider bringing a sidekick to hold the timer and say, "On your mark . . . get set . . . go!")

FOR INVISIBILITY: Stand as still and as silent as you can. Focus on your breathing: in and out, in and out. Allow your thoughts to melt away, and as they do, allow yourself to also melt away. Practice 2 hours every day until you can become invisible in under 2 seconds.

NOTE: FOR A COMPLETE LIST OF DEVELOPMENTAL EXERCISES, CONSULT *SUPERFIT* FROM THE READING LIST ON PAGE 130

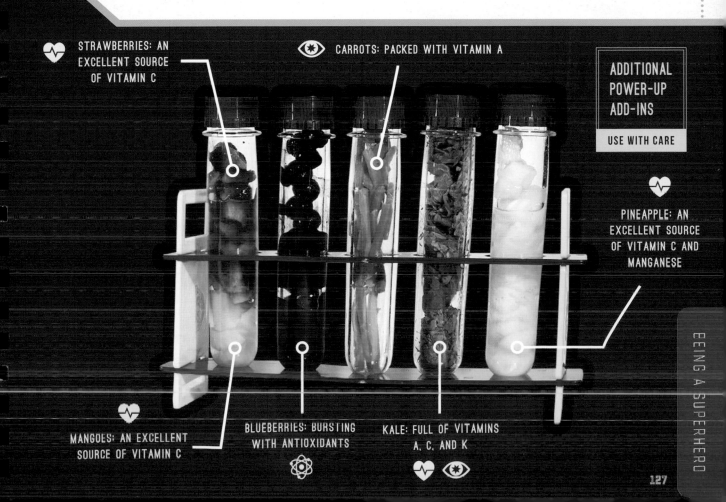

STRAWBERRIES: AN EXCELLENT SOURCE OF VITAMIN C

CARROTS: PACKED WITH VITAMIN A

ADDITIONAL POWER-UP ADD-INS

USE WITH CARE

PINEAPPLE: AN EXCELLENT SOURCE OF VITAMIN C AND MANGANESE

MANGOES: AN EXCELLENT SOURCE OF VITAMIN C

BLUEBERRIES: BURSTING WITH ANTIOXIDANTS

KALE: FULL OF VITAMINS A, C, AND K

5B TRAINING TO BE A SUPERHERO

5B.1 CAMP SUPER

The first choice for most novice superheroes—especially the younger ones—is Camp Super. Held every year in an undisclosed location, Camp Super runs would-be superheroes through all the basics: your secret identity, dealing with villains, being a good citizen, and of course, how to get those tights on as quickly (and comfortably) as possible. When their time at Camp Super is up, superheroes can leap a building like the best of them and have acquired lifelong friends (and rivalries).

SUPER BADGES

RESCUE   SECRET IDENTITY   VILLAINS   CITIZENSHIP

THE VILLAIN IN THE TREE
(To the tune of "On Top of Spaghetti")

On top of a mountain,
Inside of a tree,
A villain was hiding
And waiting for me.

His gun was a-blazing
With laser-red light,
And then the dark villain
Caught me in his sights.

He pulled the trigger,
But to his surprise
I leapt to the heavens
And flew through the skies.

Before he knew it
My fists left their place
And with cracking contact
Flew into his face.

He grunted and staggered
And fell to the ground,
And with my lasso
I hog-tied him down.

The cops came to get him
And his face turned pale.
They loaded him quickly
To take him to jail.

He glowered and shouted
And cursed back at me,
But I was napping
Inside of his tree.

THE HERO'S ANTHEM
(To the tune of "Home on the Range")

Oh give me a mask, and a difficult task,
And villains as far as you see
With mobs on the run, and odds ten to one—
It's the life of a hero for me!

CHORUS:
Oh, oh to be me!
With the power to save and set free.
I can win all the fights. I can do it in tights.
It's the life of a hero for me!

The evil is dark, and our backs have a mark,
And the villains are swarming like bees.
There's a bomb at the bank, and a nut in a tank—
It's the life of a hero for me!

—CHORUS—

The robots invade, and the aliens raid,
And the monster is covered in fleas.
But I have no fear, and can dodge like a deer—
It's the life of a hero for me!

—CHORUS—

Camp songs from Camp Super have been a tradition (and have been infuriating to villains) since they were first used in 1923.

Train regularly, or you'll be in this unenviable position.

5B.2 ONGOING TRAINING

In addition to attending a super training program like Camp Super, it's essential to keep your skills sharp through regular ongoing training. Exercise, mock combat sessions, drills, and a steady diet of books and information are all critical components to a good training regimen.

5B.3 DAILY EXERCISE ROUTINE

As a superhero, you need to maintain above-human speed, strength, and agility. Here's a possible workout plan, but feel free to up the weight or the number of reps if it seems too easy.

3 LAPS AROUND THE CITY

300 PUSHUPS

1-MILE SPRINTS (50 REPS)

200 ONE-ARMED PULL-UPS, EACH ARM

BENCH PRESS WITH A BUS (50 REPS)

500 CRUNCHES

5C DEVELOPING YOUR BRAND

5C.1 DESIGNING A LOGO

At the center of your superhero brand is your logo. Make it clear and bold, with a striking central image that will bring fear to the hearts of your enemies.

RECOMMENDED:

NOT RECOMMENDED:

5C.2 MAKE YOUR OWN LOGO

Logo Design Tips

- Make your logo large and easy to see. Fill most of the circle if you can.
- Use contrasting colors so your logo pops. Examples include red and yellow, blue and orange, or black and white.
- Keep it simple. A complicated image or lots of text can make it hard to see who you are.
- Don't copy! Your logo must be yours and yours alone.

As your popularity grows, you might consider selling these in the frozen foods aisle. Just don't let the success go to your head! (see page 150)

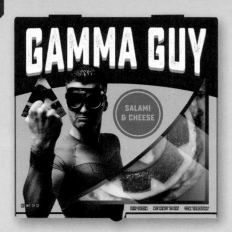

GAMMA GUY

SALAMI & CHEESE

5C.3 SUPER LOGO PIZZAS

If you want to take your super logo to new heights, try making it into a personal pizza. Use salami, cheese, vegetables, or anything you'd like to transform the top into a super snack.

SUPPLIES:

1 jar (16 ounces) pizza sauce

1/4 cup fresh, grated parmesan cheese

1 teaspoon Italian seasoning

Salt and pepper to taste

12 whole wheat flatbreads or tortillas

1 cup shredded mozzarella cheese

12 salami slices (2–3 inches)

Assorted cheese slices

Bell peppers, various colors

Assorted veggies of choice, chopped or sliced

MISSION:

1 Preheat oven to 425 degrees. Spray two cookie sheets with non-stick spray and set aside until ready to use.

2 Mix pizza sauce, parmesan cheese, and spices in a medium bowl and stir until combined. Spread evenly on each flatbread.

3 Cover the flatbreads with the mozzarella cheese. Top each pizza with your own super-hero logo designs created from salami and cheese slices cut into various shapes and assorted chopped and sliced veggies.

4 Bake for 12 to 15 minutes or until cheese is melted and lightly browned.

5 Remove from oven and cool pan on wire rack for 5 minutes before removing to serve.

MAKES 12 MINI PIZZAS

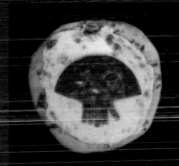
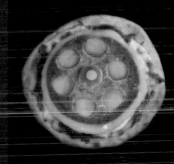

5C.4 CATCHPHRASES

Most superheroes are known for having a snazzy catch-phrase. These are rarely trademarked, but it's still best to come up with something original. Take a look at the ideas below, then try your hand at writing some ideas of your own. When you're finished, practice saying it several times in front of the mirror. Be sure to give it plenty of umph!

CATCHPHRASE TIPS:

- Try adding alliteration (i.e., use words that start with the same letter) or a form of rhyme.
- Use powerful words like *crush* and *ka-pow*.
- Keep it short and simple so it doesn't take long to say.

TEST CATCHPHRASES

That's one step for me, one building-sized leap for justice!

Ka-POW, punk!

Never cross a super boss!

Crime-fighting . . . it's what I do!

Power up, buttercup!

For truth, justice, and free ice cream for all!

Zoom, zoom and boom-chicka-boom!

Into the sky we fly, we fly!

Heeeeere's JUSTICE!

Rain or shine, day or night, when evil comes, we fight, fight, fight!

Time to crush some evil!

WRITE YOUR OWN

Time to bite you!

Kill time

Fight

Super. v. Villiah

Are you classy? A bit rogue? How you groom says a lot about what you stand for as a hero. Since most of you is covered in a suit and mask, we'll focus on the basics: hair and teeth.

COMMON SUPERHERO HAIRSTYLES

CLASSIC CURL
Always in style and always stays in place (even after multidimensional travel).

WIND SWEPT
Trendy, messy look, but ideal for flying supers who find their hair gets messed up a lot.

FAUX FLIP
Popular among the younger superheroes but discouraged for ranking heroes.

FIGHTING FRO
Makes a strong statement, but a bit cumbersome when it comes to wearing a mask.

POWER PERM
Tight, conservative, and battle-friendly. Best choice if wearing a fitted or complicated mask.

DARING DONUTS
Unconventional, but creates two perfect compartments for carrying extra ammo.

BOOM BOOM BANGS
Generally scorned since the 1970s, but a strong statement if paired with the right boots.

CIVILIAN CUT
Less stylish than other cuts, but an excellent way to blend in. Ideal for many aliases.

KEEPING YOUR SUPER SMILE

If you want to flash your super smile, you'll need to keep it clean and healthy. Floss, brush, and be sure to see your dentist regularly.

FLOSS DAILY

SUPER FLOSS

SUPER PASTE

BRUSH AT LEAST TWICE DAILY

VISIT A DENTIST REGULARLY

50.1 FINDING THE RIGHT SIDEKICK MATTERS

Saving the world can be a big, lonely job, so many heroes choose to enlist a sidekick. Be warned, though— you don't want to end up with "that guy."

A GOOD SIDEKICK:

- Anticipates your moves, needs, and strategies
- Will take a bullet for you
- Can complete your sentences and catch-phrases
- Knows when to be quiet
- Is fiercely loyal
- Complements your superpowers with her own skills

A BAD SIDEKICK:

- Complains about his suit, his pay, his equipment, his assignments, his mom, his pet cat . . .
- Runs at the first sign of trouble
- Forgets vital mission plans
- Talks your ear off
- "Borrows" your gear
- Confuses the ends of a ray gun

SIDEKICK FUMBLES

December 1—Nimbus's latest side-kick, Earth Mover, has done it again. In a sting operation against Dr. Freeze, Earth Mover confused the freeze ray's on switch with the off switch and successfully froze Nimbus in four feet of ice while Dr. Freeze escaped. Nimbus is advertising for a new sidekick. If interested,

50.2 CONDUCTING AN INTERVIEW

A sidekick should be brave, loyal, and resourceful, but there are several other factors you should consider, so when you interview a potential candidate, be sure to ask the right questions.

- If I am stuck in quicksand, what two items will you pull from your utility belt?
- How do you feel about being used as bait?
- If/when your mind is taken over by a supervillain, how much will you resent me if I am forced to incapacitate you?
- Do you have aspirations to become a hero with a sidekick of your own someday?
- Do you look best in canary yellow, hunter green, or candy-apple red?
- Can you operate heavy machinery (e.g., forklift, bulldozer, steamroller, etc.)?
- When I am discouraged about the inevitability of evil in the world, what joke would you tell to lighten the mood?
- Are you an orphan or a ward of the state?
- If chosen, what will be your snappy catchphrase? ("Holy _____!" is already taken.)
- When facing a large monster, what kind of distraction would you create to give me time to make my move?
- What is my favorite flavor of ice cream? (A sidekick must know these things.)

APPLICANT LOCATIONS

50.3 WHERE TO FIND SIDEKICK APPLICANTS

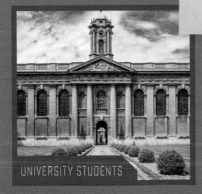
UNIVERSITY STUDENTS

ELITE POLICE FORCES

DO-GOODER CLUBS

CAMP SUPER, OF COURSE

FORMER SOLDIERS

THE CIRCUS

50.4 SIDEKICK SALAD WITH CROUTONS

SUPPLIES:

SALAD

1/2 head iceberg lettuce, chopped into 1/8-inch-wide strips

1/2 head romaine lettuce, chopped into 1/8-inch-wide strips

1/4 cup basil, torn into small pieces

3 cups shredded mozzarella cheese

1 cup garbanzo beans

4 cups cherry tomatoes

CROUTONS

4–5 whole grain or flaxseed flatbreads or pitas

2 tablespoons olive oil

2 tablespoons butter

Salt and pepper, to taste

1/2 teaspoon Italian seasoning

MISSION:

SALAD

1 Toss all ingredients with your favorite dressing together in a large bowl and serve with croutons.

SERVES 6

CROUTONS

1 Cut out six croutons from flatbreads or pitas with a 2- to 3-inch gingerbread boy cookie cutter. Place each on a baking sheet lined with parchment paper. Set aside until ready to use.

2 Preheat oven to 350 degrees. Melt the butter and olive oil in a microwave-safe bowl. Add salt and pepper to taste and Italian seasoning. Stir to blend.

3 Brush each bread cutout with olive oil mixture and bake 8 to 10 minutes.

4 Remove from oven, cool, and serve with salad.

MAKES 6 CROUTONS

PRESENTATION IDEA

To make a hit at your next superhero reunion, try serving the salads in individual glasses. Decorate each one with your favorite superheroes' (or sidekicks') logos. Here are some helpful ideas:

- Create colored bands by gluing colored strips of felt or placing colored rubber bands around the rim of each cup.
- Attach colored napkins or tissue paper to make capes.
- Create logos out of colored felt or foam paper and glue them to one of the colored bands.

50.5 GOING SOLO

Even the pop stars know that there comes a time when working as a team just isn't, well, working. As a superhero, you might have a brilliant entourage of other supers, sidekicks, techies, butlers, friends, animals, and even robots working with you, but at a certain point, it might be better to fight crime all by your onesie.

How do you know when it's time to go solo? Take the "Is It Time to Go Solo?" quiz, of course.

IS IT TIME TO GO SOLO?

- Are you constantly having to put your life and the safety of the city in jeopardy to save your sidekick or another member of your team?

- Do some members of your team want to change your team colors? (You might call this "artistic differences.")

- Did your sidekick fall into a vat of toxic waste and suddenly gain powers that might just be cooler than yours?

- Do some members of the team refuse to sing backup for your songs on super karaoke night?

- Are you fond of brooding alone on top of tall buildings at night?

- Did your sidekick forget your birthday last year?

If you answered "yes" to two or more of the above questions, consider heading in a new direction. You might be better off working alone.

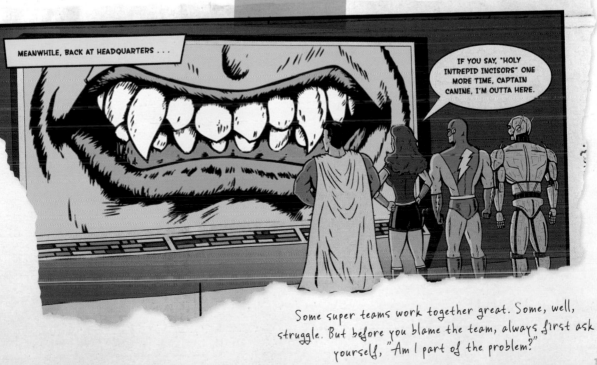

Some super teams work together great. Some, well, struggle. But before you blame the team, always first ask yourself, "Am I part of the problem?"

SOCIAL MEDIA

With the rise of social media, fans have taken to the web to learn more about their favorite superheroes. From live tweeting during battles to flying selfies, many superheroes are embracing the social media scene and the support they receive from their friends and followers online. Smart superheroes know how to get all the benefits of social media without falling prey to the dangers.

5E.1 SOCIAL MEDIA DOS AND DON'TS FOR SUPERHEROES

DO

DON'T

#NoFilter

DO protect your secret identity. (Filters don't count as masks.)

DO use social media to connect with other supers.

 GammaGuy
@GammaGuy

Nice work defeating those giant space monkeys, @Galactigirl #YoureMyHero #SuperheroGoals

DO respond kindly to the outpouring of love from random fans.

 Brooke Jorden I love you, Gamma Guy! Thank you for saving the city!

 Gamma Guy No, thank YOU, random citizen!

4.5M 👍

Who has the most friends? #ThisGuy 👍

DON'T let the number of friends, followers, likes, or favorites your super profile has go to your head. (Remember, Facebook "friends" are not the same as real friends— real friends buy you pizza.)

DON'T share pictures of your food OR gym selfies (or selfies of you eating at the gym). You're better than that!

#SUPERfood #FitFam

DON'T spend all your time scrolling through social media sites. Get out there and save some lives!

5F YOUR SECRET HIDEOUT

Your secret hideout is a place to hide from enemies, prepare for battles, keep track of villains, store your equipment, and get some rest and relaxation.

AERIAL VIEW OF SECRET COMPOUND

Most superheroes keep their secret hideout underground, sometimes with a compound aboveground to match their alias identity. If you do opt for such an arrangement, here is a possible layout:

1   Main house, preferably with an interior entrance to your secret hideout. (Note: Hideouts should have several entrance options. See below for additional entrance ideas.)

2   Garage (also a good place to put your sidekick on bad days).

3   Pool (with helicopter launch pad hidden underneath).

4   Umbrella (with defense lasers).

5   Landscaping for privacy (a few fake trees should double as Internet and radio receivers).

RECOMMENDED ENTRANCE DISGUISES

WATERFALLS

ABANDONED MINES

PORTA-POTTIES

LEVERED BOOKCASES

A Note about Intruders

If your secret hideout does get compromised and you can't successfully defend it, follow this procedure:

1. Wipe your central computer (make sure you've saved a data backup somewhere).
2. Destroy all weapons stored.
3. Seal all entrances and exits (after you're out, of course).
4. Find a superhero friend whose couch you can sleep on for a while.
5. Rebuild!

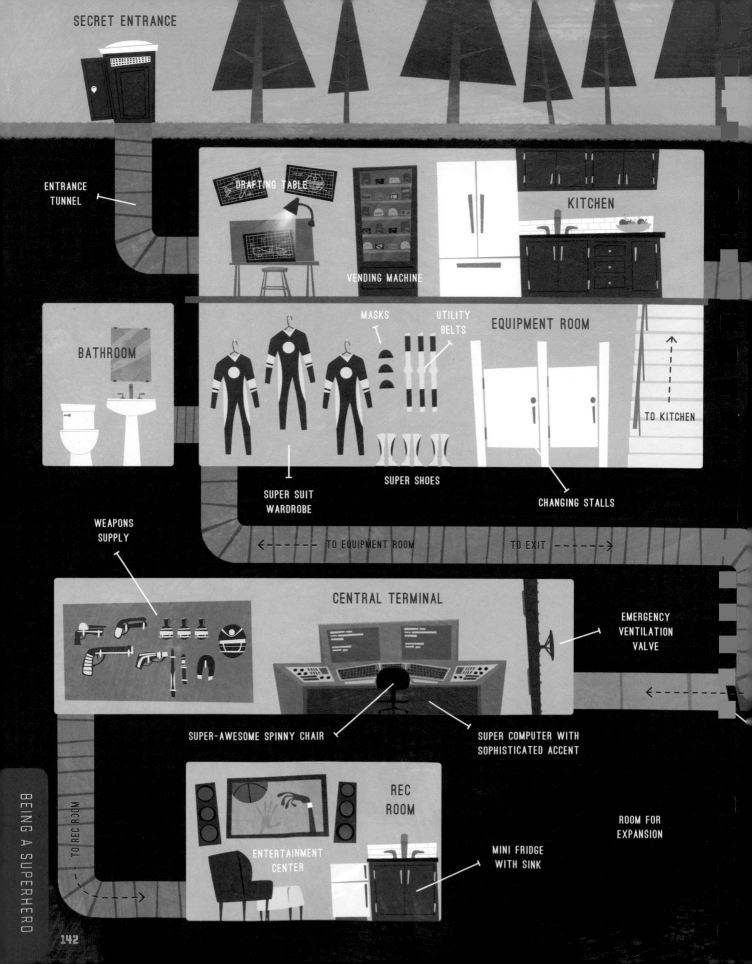

SECRET ENTRANCE

ENTRANCE
TUNNEL

DRAFTING TABLE

VENDING MACHINE

KITCHEN

BATHROOM

MASKS

UTILITY
BELTS

EQUIPMENT ROOM

TO KITCHEN

SUPER SUIT
WARDROBE

SUPER SHOES

CHANGING STALLS

WEAPONS
SUPPLY

← - - - - - - - TO EQUIPMENT ROOM   TO EXIT - - - - - →

CENTRAL TERMINAL

EMERGENCY
VENTILATION
VALVE

SUPER-AWESOME SPINNY CHAIR

SUPER COMPUTER WITH
SOPHISTICATED ACCENT

REC
ROOM

ROOM FOR
EXPANSION

ENTERTAINMENT
CENTER

MINI FRIDGE
WITH SINK

TO REC ROOM

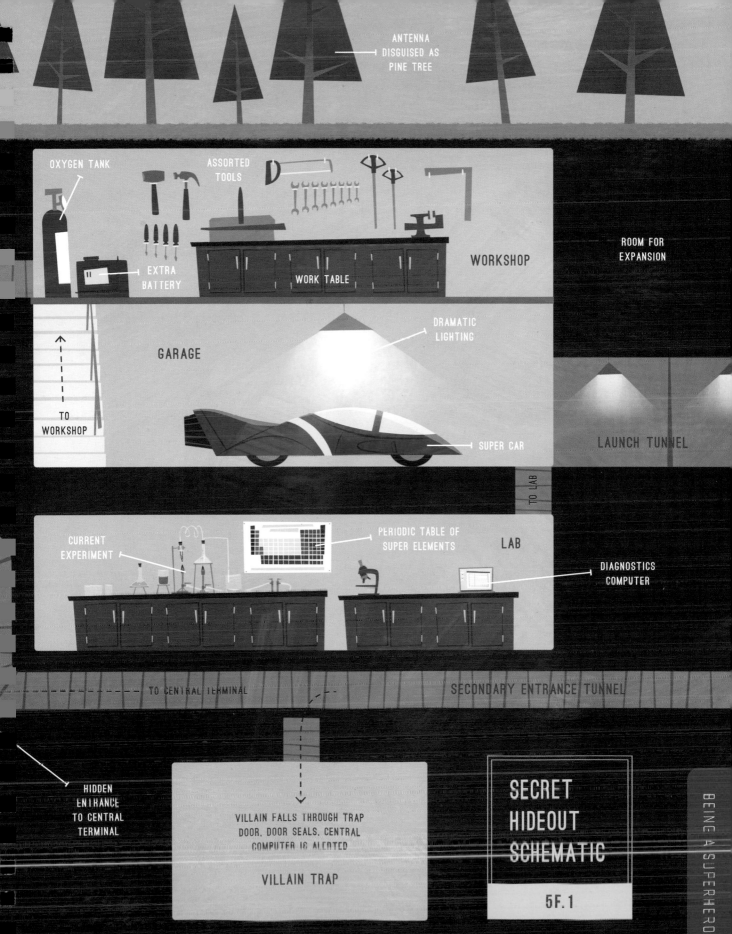

ANTENNA
DISGUISED AS
PINE TREE

OXYGEN TANK

ASSORTED
TOOLS

ROOM FOR
EXPANSION

WORKSHOP

EXTRA
BATTERY

WORK TABLE

DRAMATIC
LIGHTING

GARAGE

TO
WORKSHOP

SUPER CAR

LAUNCH TUNNEL

TO LAB

CURRENT
EXPERIMENT

PERIODIC TABLE OF
SUPER ELEMENTS

LAB

DIAGNOSTICS
COMPUTER

TO CENTRAL TERMINAL

SECONDARY ENTRANCE TUNNEL

HIDDEN
ENTRANCE
TO CENTRAL
TERMINAL

VILLAIN FALLS THROUGH TRAP
DOOR, DOOR SEALS, CENTRAL
COMPUTER IS ALERTED

VILLAIN TRAP

SECRET
HIDEOUT
SCHEMATIC

5F.1

BEING A SUPERHERO

5G BEING SUMMONED

5G.1 DIRECT HOTLINES

When duty calls, sometimes it actually calls. Many government officials use official telephone hotlines to contact superheroes when in need, and sometimes you'll need to call those officials yourself. Be sure you have the following lines installed:

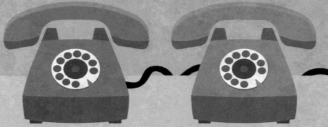

RED HOTLINE

A direct line to the desk of the President of the United States, the Prime Minister of Britain, and your mother.

BLUE HOTLINE

Connects you to the local police station, the CIA, the FBI, and MI6.

ORANGE HOTLINE

Links you to your allies at the Superhero Orbiting Station (SOS) in Sector 4.

PINK HOTLINE

A direct link to Mr. Ming's Chinese Takeout. Hungry heroes are a national emergency, after all.

#47-E SPOTLIGHT SIGNAL EXAMPLES

When communications are down, or if you're interested in something with more flair, a spotlight signal can be a good way to go. Help a civilian you trust (a police chief or fire chief, for example) install a spotlight signal in a convenient location. Note: This kind of communication only works at night, so you're advised to have a daylight method as well.

5G.3 MAKE YOUR OWN MINI SPOTLIGHT SIGNAL

If mounting a giant spotlight to the roof of the police station seems a little conspicuous, try making a miniature version that can be kept in a desk or briefcase.

SUPPLIES:

A flashlight (with batteries!)

Duct tape, preferably black (but traditional silver is okay)

Scissors

Sketch of your superhero logo (see page 131) for reference

Fine-tipped permanent marker

MISSION:

1 Place the lens end of a flashlight flat on a piece of paper with the flashlight standing up.

2 Trace around the lens with a marker. Remove the flashlight so you have a clean circle on your paper, roughly the same size as the flashlight's lens.

3 Carefully draw your superhero logo in the center of the circle. Make sure it's large, but leave plenty of space between it and the circle's edge so that the light can shine around it.

Tip: If your logo is complicated, we recommend simplifying it a bit so that the shape is easier to cut out and attach onto your light.

---

4 Cut out your paper logo.

5 Cut off a piece of duct tape that's at least as long as the diameter of the flashlight's lens. Lay it sticky-side up on a table. Lightly place your paper logo on top of the tape—try not to let it stick.

6 Carefully trace around the paper logo onto the tape with the marker. Remove the paper and cut out the logo from the tape.

7 Stick the tape logo onto the lens of your flashlight. Turn off the lights, turn on the flashlight, and shine your special signal on the wall!

TAPE

LENS

SAMPLE LENS LOGO DESIGNS

BEING A SUPER-HER

HANDLING FAME AND FORTUNE

Being a hero means everything that comes with it, and that includes fame, fortune, and honors. This collection will give you a sense of what you should be prepared for, and the following section will help you know how to best handle it.

5H.1 COMMON AWARDS, COMMENDATIONS, AND CONTRACTS

OFFICIAL LETTERS OF COMMENDATION

CITY OF COASTVILLE

Dear Cyclostorm,

Thank you for once again saving our city. We thought nothing could be worse than the giant electric eels that wrapped themselves around the high-rises last week, but the one-eyed, photon-firing robot you defeated this week could have completely destroyed the city. You have our deepest appreciation. In fact, if your schedule allows it, we would like to present you with the key to the city at a grand ceremony tomorrow afternoon. Please let us know if you will be available.

Regards,

Mayor Wyatt Watson and the city of Coastville

P.S. If it's not too much trouble, could you try not to crash through quite so many buildings while you battle these supervillains? Not that we're ungrateful, but our budget is running a bit low with all of the reconstruction.

MEDALS

HERO OF THE YEAR AWARD

1987

STATUE DEDICATED

Sydney—Government officials presided over the dedication of a statue of Wonder Wombat, the city's hero. Overlooking the harbor, Wombat's eternal tribute to his

STATUES & MONUMENTS

SANGER STUDIOS PRESENTS A BARBARA BEERY FILM BY CONNER ROBBINS TAYLOR ROBBINS KIENAN ROBBINS CAMERON ROBBINS JOSHUA ROBBINS
SCREENPLAY BY ERIKA RIGGS EDITED BY BROOKE JORDEN MUSIC BY CODA PRODUCTION DESIGNER DAVID MILES COSTUME DESIGN BY ML DESIGN ANIMAL HANDLER SARAH ROBBINS
STUNTS BY CHRISTIAN ROBBINS EXECUTIVE PRODUCERS CHRISTOPHER ROBBINS MICHELE ROBBINS

RAINBOY
RETURNS

IT'S ABOUT
TO GET
STORMY

IN THEATERS NOVE

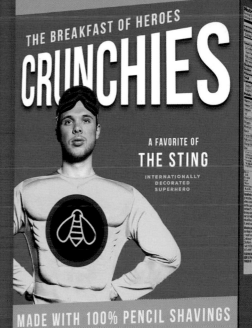

THE BREAKFAST OF HEROES

CRUNCHIES

A FAVORITE OF
THE STING

INTERNATIONALLY
DECORATED
SUPERHERO

MADE WITH 100% PENCIL SHAVINGS

NT WT 16 OZ

PRODUCT ENDORSEMENTS

COMIC BOOK SERIES

DWM COMICS GROUP

47 JUNE 03975 20¢

HE'S BACK, AND HE'S ANGRY!

APPROVED BY THE COMICS CODE AUTHORITY

CAPTAIN CAPTION

TAKES ON THE JADED JOURNALIST

THIS WILL
TEACH YOU
NOT TO
PLAGIARIZE!

SHOULD YOU GET AN AGENT?

If your fame is such that you start receiving requests to use your likeness in movies, comic books, television commercials, and radio shows, you might want to consider getting an agent to help handle your arrangements and contracts. Be sure you find someone you trust. Also, take care to not let your public appearances prevent you from fulfilling your most important duty: saving the world.

5H.2 MAKE YOUR OWN COMIC BOOK

One of the greatest sources of fame a superhero will ever encounter is the comic book. Your heroic deeds—and your mishaps—will all be recorded in stunning color for future generations to enjoy. If you haven't been contacted for a comic book deal yet, here's an easy way to make your own.

SUPPLIES:

White paper

Pens, pencils, crayons, colored pencils, markers

Fine-tipped black marker

Stapler

MISSION:

1 With the help of a parent, visit www.familius.com/the-ultimate-guide-to-being-a-superhero. Click the link called "Comic Book Template." Print as many copies of this as you'd like (we recommend no more than eight, or the book will be too hard to staple). Be sure to print them double sided.

> **Tip:** If you have trouble printing the pages double sided, just print one page off and take it to a copy store or library. Someone there can help you make double-sided photocopies of your page for the rest of your comic book.

2 Stack the pages on top of each other. Then, add a blank piece of paper to the bottom of the stack (this will serve as your comic book's cover). Make sure all the edges line up.

3 Carefully staple down the dotted line, right in the center of the pages. Keep the staples running in the same direction as the line. You'll need at least three staples to hold the book together: one at the top, one in the middle, and one at the bottom. Adding more staples will strengthen the binding. If your stapler can't reach into the middle of the paper, unhinge the stapler and carefully press the staples in that way. Then, turn the book over and flatten the staple ends down.

4 Fold the book in half along the line of staples. Crease the binding by pushing your fingers along it several times.

5 Your book is ready! Decide which of your stupendous adventures you want to tell, design the cover, then fill in each of the interior frames with all the details, characters, and dialogue you need. Don't hold back—make your story as exciting as possible!

COMIC BOOK TIPS

Plan your book out first. Decide how many frames you'll use to tell the beginning, middle, and end of the story.

Put the dialogue in speech bubbles or plain white boxes. This will make it more readable.

Outline your drawings with a black, fine-tipped marker. This will help your drawings pop and keep your colors clear.

8 PAGES (PRINTED ON BOTH SIDES)

STAPLE DOWN THE MIDDLE

FLATTEN STAPLES, FOLD INTO BOOK

5H.3 HOW TO AVOID EGOPLASIA

Remember to keep your ego in check or you might be at risk of developing egoplasia. Despite the awards and adoring fans, your true motivation should always be battling evil and protecting the innocent. Always keep yourself grounded by maintaining friendships with ordinary people. Treat your fans with kindness and respect. And for goodness' sake, leave the politics to the politicians.

CASE STUDY: CAPTAIN COOL

Captain Cool (alias: Reginald Toupe) is a perfect, and unfortunate, case study in egoplasia. His rising fame led to speaking engagements, advertising contracts, and his own line of athletic gear. Friends first noticed symptoms of egoplasia when Cool allowed a movie to be made of his career—and he played the role of himself. Symptoms only worsened, developing into increased risk-taking, an obsession with hair gel, and a head the size of a beach ball. Cool met his downfall when a villain attacked from behind during one of his speeches. Cool was so busy listing his own achievements that he never even heard the ray gun.

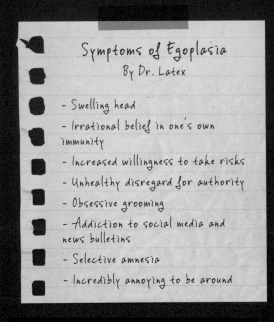

Symptoms of Egoplasia
By Dr. Latex

- Swelling head
- Irrational belief in one's own immunity
- Increased willingness to take risks
- Unhealthy disregard for authority
- Obsessive grooming
- Addiction to social media and news bulletins
- Selective amnesia
- Incredibly annoying to be around

CIVILIAN PROFILE: DR. LATEX

Sarcastic and ill-tempered, Dr. Latex is nevertheless a medical genius and the chief physician for most superheroes. It is widely believed that Earth is not really his home planet, but no one has dared to ask.

ASSESSMENT ANSWER KEY

Find which column had the highest total of checkmarks. Match the letter of that column to your description below:

(A) Sadly, you are suffering from egoplasia. Fame has caught you in its tempting grip, and the only way out is to do something so completely embarrassing that you'll be forced to eat a slice of humble pie. **(B)** You may have a sliver of humility left, but beware: your ego is growing. Be sure to spend a few minutes each day looking at your school pictures from junior high. That should be enough to keep you humble. **(C)** It's okay to bask in the glow of your own fame occasionally, but never indulge too much to lose sight of your own weaknesses. **(D)** Good for you! You don't dwell on your fame, and that makes you both wise and awesome. Keep up the good work! **(E)** Great news: you don't have The Big Head. But now we're starting to wonder if you are actually a superhero at all . . .

EGOPLASIA SELF-ASSESSMENT TEST

It can happen to the best superheroes—fame tends to go to our heads. But how can you know whether your head has swollen to the size of your home planet? Consider each of these questions and place a checkmark in the column that best describes you. Then, tally the number of checkmarks in each column and match it to the Assessment Answer Key on page 150.

QUESTION	Multiple times a day	Once a day	Occasionally	Seldom	Never
1 How often do you Google yourself?				✓	
2 How often do you count the number of honorary degrees you've received?		✓			
3 How often do you flex in front of the mirror?					✓
4 How often do you practice making a fancy signature?			✓		
5 How often do you talk about yourself in the third person?				✓	
6 How often do you express your political views in public?					✓
7 How often do you refer to non-supers as "the little people"?					✓
8 How often do you check the number of followers you have on social media?					✓
NUMBER OF CHECKMARKS:					
	A	B	C	D	E

YOUR COMMITMENT TO THE WORLD

51.1 THE MAKING OF A REAL HERO

The true measure of a superhero is not strength or superpowers. Being a superhero isn't about the fame and the fan clubs and the cool gadgets. No, a superhero must be brave enough to stand up in the face of evil and fight for justice.

Armed with the knowledge and skills outlined in this book, it is your responsibility to live up to your superhero potential. Make a commitment to yourself—and your city—that you will serve your community and save those in need of saving. Fighting crime can be a tough and lonely job, but a true hero puts others first by selflessly serving those who need help.

Look around you: Many people need your protection. Others need your support and encouragement. Still others simply need your kindness. Not all heroic acts happen on the battlefield.

Be a true hero!

#KL7-1 REAL SUPERS SPEAK ABOUT THE QUALITIES OF TRUE HEROES

COURAGE "SUCCESS IS NOT FINAL, FAILURE IS NOT FATAL: IT IS THE COURAGE TO CONTINUE THAT COUNTS." —WINSTON S. CHURCHILL

OPTIMISM "IN SPITE OF EVERYTHING, I STILL BELIEVE THAT PEOPLE ARE REALLY GOOD AT HEART." —ANNE FRANK

HONESTY "WHOEVER IS CARELESS WITH THE TRUTH IN SMALL MATTERS CANNOT BE TRUSTED WITH IMPORTANT MATTERS." —ALBERT EINSTEIN

LOYALTY "MASTER, GO ON, AND I WILL FOLLOW THEE TO THE LAST GASP WITH TRUTH AND LOYALTY." —WILLIAM SHAKESPEARE

KINDNESS "BE KIND, FOR EVERYONE YOU MEET IS FIGHTING A HARDER BATTLE." —PLATO

SERVICE "THOSE WHO ARE HAPPIEST ARE THOSE WHO DO THE MOST FOR OTHERS." —BOOKER T. WASHINGTON

TEAMWORK "ALONE WE CAN DO SO LITTLE; TOGETHER WE CAN DO SO MUCH." —HELEN KELLER

HUMILITY "A GREAT MAN IS ALWAYS WILLING TO BE LITTLE." —RALPH WALDO EMERSON

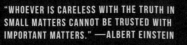

The Superhero Pledge

As a superhero, I solemnly promise:

To use my powers for good, never for evil.

To treat all people with respect — whether they be supers or civilians.

To protect the innocent and those who cannot protect themselves.

To be an example of service in my community.

To stand for truth, justice, and peace.

Arjun. Mahesh. Gopalan

Superhero's Signature

By signing The Superhero Pledge, you are joining the ranks of brave men and women who have safeguarded truth and justice for thousands of years. Take a good look at their portraits. These are large shoes to fill, but broad shoulders to stand on.

THE WIZ AND FLEXCALIBUR

(Alias: Merlin and King Arthur) This famous super-sidekick duo protected Britain for years with the help of a band of superheroes, a famous sword, and a perfectly round table.

AXEMAN

(Alias: George Washington) Honest to a fault, Axeman led a young United States through its war with Great Britain. In his most famous victory (pictured here), Axeman's laser vision successfully thawed the Delaware River and allowed his army to cross.

POLONIUM

(Alias: Marie Curie) Superbly gifted in chemistry and physics, Polonium pioneered the use of radiation and X-rays for supers without X-ray vision. She put these skills to good use by X-raying soldiers during World War I.

GRAVITON

(Alias: Isaac Newton) The first superhero to identify the force of gravity, which was an essential first step to understanding why some supers (including himself) couldn't stay aloft for more than 3 seconds.

FLORENTIAN

(Alias: Leonardo Da Vinci) Brilliantly talented in countless areas, Florentian equipped the superheroes of the 15th century with cutting-edge inventions, weapons, and portraits. The painting of his sidekick, Lisamona, has enchanted the public to this day.

STARGAZER

(Alias: Galileo Galilei) Vitally instrumental in pioneering modern-day astronomy and detecting space anomalies indicative of invading aliens.

WINDY LINDY

(Alias: Amelia Earhart) Widely considered the most gifted—and adventurous—superhero with the power of flight. Her mysterious disappearence has never been fully explained.

QUILLDRIVER

(Alias: William Shakespeare) Playwright by day, super by night, Quilldriver protected the city streets of London until his death in 1616. His superhero experience inspired many of his plays, including "A Midsummer Night's Scream" and "Merchant of Menace."

THE ORCHESTRATOR

(Alias: Ludwig van Beethoven) Endowed with supervision and supersound, The Orchestrator ran a secret team of supers from under his performance hall in Vienna. To keep his cover, he feigned deafness for most of his life and also composed a number of groundbreaking symphonies. Villains and supers alike begged him to write their personal soundtracks, but to no avail.

MR. MUSCLES

(Alias: Spartacus) Led a slave revolt against the Roman government. Though unsuccessful, his valor has inspired superheroes for centuries.

CHARACTER GUIDE

CIVILIANS

CHRISTOPHER CARDALL
Page 27

DR. LATEX
Page 150

VILLAINS

THE TERMIGATOR
Page 39

THE PAJAMA MASTER
Page 39

DR. DIABOLICAL
Page 39

PROFESSOR A
Page 43

CALAMITY BANE
Page 45

DR. FREEZE
Page 58

LIP BOMB
Page 69

SUPERHEROES

TORNATOR
Page 12

ALDENTE
Page 18

STAGEHAND
Page 53

DEWEY DECIMATOR
Page 56

DOUBLE TIME
Page 89

NIMBUS
Page 99

SIGHTS
Page 103

RAINBOY
Page 125

GREEN THUMB
Page 125

HANDSTAND
Page 125

BACONATOR
Page 125

MISS CANINE
Page 125

CAPTAIN COOL
Page 150

RECIPE GUIDE

CRAFT GUIDE

SUPERHERO MASK
Page 16

PHONE BOOTH
Page 25

IDENTITY CARDS
Page 32

MIND CONTROL-
PREVENTION HELMET
Page 65

TRAINING-GRADE
BLACK SLIME
Page 67

DESIGN YOUR OWN
SUPERSUIT
Page 72

T-SHIRT CAPE
Page 74

WRIST CUFFS
Page 77

GLOVES
Page 78

SUPERSHOES
Page 79

UTILITY BELT
Page 82

SUPERVISION
PERISCOPE
Page 84

SUPERSHIELD
Page 86

SUPER SPEED
GRIP SOCKS
Page 88

HIGH-RISE BUILDING
BLOCKS
Page 111

PUNCHING BAG
PILLOW
Page 115

MAKE YOUR OWN
LOGO
Page 131

MINI SPOTLIGHT
SIGNAL
Page 145

COMIC BOOK
Page 148

ABOUT THE CREATORS

THE WICKED WHISK (ALIAS: BARBARA BEERY, AUTHOR)

Children's cooking expert by day, hunger-fighting hero by night, The Wicked Whisk is the bestselling author of *The Pink Princess Cookbook*. She has been a spokesperson for such national companies as Sun Maid Raisin, Uncle Ben's, Borden's, Kellogg's Rice Krispies, and Step 2, and has appeared twice on the *Today Show* and the CBN with Pat Robertson. Her business has been featured in the *New York Times* and *Entrepreneur Magazine*, as well as dozens of other local and national publications. The Wicked Whisk has worked closely with Get Moving, Cookies for Kids' Cancer, Rachael Ray's Yum-O! organization, and No Kids Hungry. She is the author of twelve books, having sold more than 500,000 copies, and resides in Austin, Texas, in a secure and secret location.

THE OXFORD COMET (ALIAS: BROOKE JORDEN, AUTHOR)

Armed with the Red Pencil of Truth and the Eraser of Justice, the Oxford Comet defends the world—and its books—from the evils of bland prose and misplaced modifiers. In her down time, she orbits the world with her husband, their daughter, and their cat.

BOOKPLATE (ALIAS: DAVID MILES, AUTHOR AND DESIGNER)

Bookplate makes a living creating books for superheroes worldwide. He also reads books, writes books, sells books, shelves books, thinks about books, drives to books, sleeps to books, and cooks from books, but he doesn't eat books (which is fortunate, since that tends to wreak havoc on one's hydraulics). In addition to his underground work for superheroes, Bookplate is the author of *Book*, *Let's Count Oregon*, and *Let's Count California*. He graduated from Brigham Young University with a BS in business management and currently lives in California where he enjoys trips to Yosemite, the central coast, and the local mechanic.

JEFF-O-MAN (ALIAS: JEFF HARVEY, ILLUSTRATOR)

While working as an electrician's assistant, Jeff Harvey was fixing an electrical breaker when he touched an exposed wire. Instead of shocking him, he felt the electricity pulsing throughout his body, which he learned to use against his enemies. When not firing electrical pulses, he can be found drawing . . . and drawing . . . and drawing.

FLASH PIXEL (ALIAS: VICTORIA LEONARDO, PHOTOGRAPHER)

Flash Pixel molds light and shadow around each recipe to attract children and grown-ups alike to nutritious meals and yummy treats. With her trusty camera in hand, Flash freezes each dish in pixels to create road maps for superhero and regular cooks everywhere.

ABOUT FAMILIUS

Welcome to a place where moms and dads are celebrated, not compared. Where heart is at the center of our families, and family at the center of our homes. Where boo-boos are still kissed, cake beaters are still licked, and mistakes are still okay. Welcome to a place where books—and family—are beautiful. Familius: a book publisher dedicated to helping families be happy.

VISIT OUR WEBSITE: WWW.FAMILIUS.COM

Our website is a different kind of place. Get inspired, read articles, discover books, watch videos, connect with our family experts, download books and apps and audiobooks, and along the way, discover how values and happy family life go together.

JOIN OUR FAMILY

There are lots of ways to connect with us! Subscribe to our newsletters at www.familius.com to receive uplifting inspiration, a free ebook every month, and the first word on special discounts and Familius news.

GET BULK DISCOUNTS

If you feel a few friends and family might benefit from what you've read, let us know and we'll be happy to provide you with quantity discounts. Simply email us at orders@familius.com.

Website: www.familius.com
Facebook: www.facebook.com/paterfamilius
Twitter: @familiustalk, @paterfamilius1
Pinterest: www.pinterest.com/familius

FAMILIUS

The greatest work you ever do will be within the walls of your own home.